D0455767

Encouraging Words

ALSO BY ROBERT AITKEN

Encouraging Words

Zen Buddhist Teachings for Western Students

ROBERT AITKEN

Pantheon Books, New York and San Francisco

R0122141505
HUMCA

HOUSTON PUBLIC LIBRARY

Copyright © 1993 by Robert Aitken

All rights reserved under International and Pan-American Copyright
Conventions. Published in the United States by Pantheon Books, a
division of Random House, Inc., New York, and simultaneously in Canada
by Random House of Canada Limited, Toronto.

Portions of "Words in the Dōjō" were previously published in
Blind Donkey. "Words from the Rōshi" were previously published
in newsletters of the Diamond Sangha.

Library of Congress Cataloging-in-Publication Data
[Aitken, Robert, 1917–   ]
Encouraging words / Robert Aitken.
p.   cm.
1. Spiritual life — Zen Buddhism.   2. Zen Buddhism — Doctrines.
I. Title.
BQ9288.A35   1993
294.3'444 — dc20   92-50467

ISBN 0-679-41701-X

Book Design by Maura Fadden Rosenthal

Manufactured in the United States of America

First Edition

For Anne

Wishing to entice the blind,
The Buddha has playfully let words escape his
     golden mouth;
Heaven and earth are ever since filled with
     entangling briars.

— Daiō Kokushi
(Translated by Daisetz T. Suzuki,
Manual of Zen Buddhism)

CONTENTS

ACKNOWLEDGMENTS

First and foremost, I am grateful to my teacher, Yamada Kōun Rōshi, whose exacting guidance and compassionate trust encouraged me to stand on my own feet.

David Steinkraus helped me to edit these pieces, to arrange them in good order, and to sort out and correct the back matter. Jack Shoemaker of Pantheon Books deftly brought coherence to the manuscript with his developmental editing, and Jason Binford accordingly helped to rearrange the text and prepared the index. Nil Özbek transcribed many of the pieces, Trish Dougherty and Johanna Bangeman the others. Anne Aitken studied the penultimate draft and made cogent suggestions. It was Anne's idea to note down my extemporaneous "Words in the Dōjō," and she insisted that I record them when she was absent.

We used the occasion of preparing the manuscript of this book to revise the translations in our Daily Zen Buddhist Sutras for inclusion in the Syllabus. We held classes at Koko An to discuss some of them. Joseph Bobrow, Kazuaki Tanahashi, and Norman Waddell sent helpful recommendations from afar. Ryōzō Yamaguchi, Priest of the Myōshinji branch temple on Maui, shared his expertise generously. I am grateful to all members and friends for their loving support over the years as this book gradually came together.

Finally, I wish to acknowledge the lifework of such eminent students of Buddhism as Thomas Cleary, Daisetz T. Suzuki, and Kazuaki Tanahashi, whose translations I cite for reference. I work with less accessible texts in Chinese and Japanese as well, so my translations will sometimes differ from those cited.

R.A.
Koko An Zendō
Spring Training Period, 1992

INTRODUCTION

The establishment of Zen Buddhism in the West can be traced to Dr. Daisetz T. Suzuki's *Essays in Zen Buddhism: First Series,* published in London by Luzac in 1928. At about that same time the monk Senzaki Nyogen Sensei established the first Western Zen center in San Francisco. There had been earlier introductions, notably with the appearance of Shaku Sōen Zenji at the World Parliament of Religions in Chicago in 1892, and with the transmission of Zen and Ch'an Buddhism to the United States around the turn of the century to serve immigrant populations. It was Suzuki and Senzaki, however, who cleared the way for the naturalization of Zen as something Western. Dr. Suzuki's three volumes of essays on Zen, his *Training of a Zen Buddhist Monk, Manual of Zen Buddhism,* and other works introduced the religion to Western intellectuals, and Senzaki Sensei's teaching centers offered the way of practice. Sasaki Shigetsu Rōshi followed soon after Senzaki, and founded the Zen Buddhist Society of America in New

York, later renamed the First Zen Institute of New York. More roshis followed: Suzuki Shunryū founded the Zen Center of San Francisco in the early 1960s, and later in that same decade Sasaki Jōshū established centers in Southern California and New Mexico, Nakagawa Sōen and Yasutani Haku'un led retreats in Hawaii and on the East and West coasts of the United States, and Maezumi Haku'yū established the Zen Center of Los Angeles. These teachers and others were able to encourage the growth of a Zen movement in North America and elsewhere in the Western world. The Diamond Sangha is part of this larger movement, and was established in Honolulu in 1959. Finally, in more recent times, Korean and Vietnamese teachers have enriched the process.

As Western Zen students we have experienced certain problems during the acculturation process, some of them relating to our own perceptions and motives. It has been clear from the outset that Zen Buddhism offers understanding and strengths we missed in our own ways of life, but as we got better acquainted with our new religion, we have found that it was monastic, and perhaps not readily translatable into our egalitarian society. Certain cultural accretions are firmly embedded in the traditional way and seem unsuitable in the Western context. Our task, in relatively short order, has been to distinguish what is relevant from what is not, and to turn on some lamps that our ancestors left dark — no easy chore.

One such lamp would illuminate the lay path of marriage, children, and career. As Westerners our natural predilection is to seek ways to practice rigorously at home and in the workplace, a path some ancestral teachers thought impossible. Moreover, the unspoken understanding in the Far East has been that Zen is a practice for men. We are recasting the Dharma to include women, jobs, and family — a fascinating course with many pitfalls. A sticking point has been the lack of any specifically Buddhist moral code within the teaching of Japanese Zen masters. Though Mahayana Buddhism, the tradition of the Buddha Way found in East Asia, teaches the innate value of each being and the essential harmony of the universe, we find the Precepts of the Buddha treated metaphysically rather than practically in the Zen tradition. The old teachers turned to Confucianism, and to a lesser degree to Shinto, rather than to their own Buddhist heritage for day-to-day guidance in social affairs. As Westerners we are not as familiar with Confucianism or Shinto as we would be if we had learned of it from birth and lived within it. So we are left with the task of formulating and presenting a code of daily living as lay people that is in keeping with the basic teachings of Zen Buddhism. Much of my concern lies within this realm.

Similarly, the various traditional formulations and applications of Zen Buddhist experience have not extended very much into politics and economics. This is not just a Far Eastern lacuna but can be found throughout the history of Buddhism with a few outstanding exceptions, notably the edicts of King Ashoka and certain episodes in the life of the Buddha himself. From very early times the Buddhist Sangha stayed quite separate from worldly affairs. Then when Mahayana Buddhist missionaries moved into China, Korea, and Japan, they found indigenous religions already in place. They were permitted to establish their monasteries and practice on sufferance, and they knew they would risk their very existence if they organized for peace, social justice, or protection of the natural world in resistance to their government, if indeed such a notion ever occurred to them. Generally they took the position of many Christian leaders down through the ages, of just keeping quiet. Sometimes they would actually lend religious authority to political and economic power. When the government impinged on their lives, as it inevitably did from time to time, they would generally simply adjust to this as part of their karma.

Again there were exceptions, notably a few Korean monks who led peasant rebellions. However, broad resistance movements arising from within Buddhist orthodoxy, such as we can see today in Thailand and to some degree in the West, mark a profoundly significant shift. Times have changed. Distinctions drawn for cultural reasons between lay and clerical, and between society and the world of the spirit, have become meaningless. Monastery walls have broken down, and the old teaching and practice of wisdom, love, and responsibility are freed for the widest applications in the domain of social affairs. Thus the modern student of Zen Buddhism, or of any other form of Mahayana, Theravada, or Vajrayana Buddhism, is challenged today to maintain a balanced religious life in the temple and in the world, individually, and with like-minded friends.

This is the balance I seek in my own practice and teaching. In this book, "Words in the Dōjō" are messages to students who are meditating beneath the Bodhi tree. "Words from the Rōshi" are for those same students, but often in their context of work and play in the world. Yet the tree that shades formal religious practice also shades homemaking, schoolteaching, and building a garage. The inspiration that guided monks and nuns in the ancient Sangha is our own deepest incentive as we establish our new Sangha forms in a world that desperately needs new forms of kinship and love.

Words in the Dōjō

INTRODUCTION

"Words in the Dōjō" are edited from extemporaneous homilies I offered in retreats of Diamond Sangha centers over the years, from about 1978 to the present. Zen Buddhist retreats are called *sesshin,* a Sino-Japanese term that means primarily "to touch the mind." Sesshins are part of a traditional cycle of Zen training practiced in Far Eastern Buddhist monasteries, and have their origin in the monsoon retreats of early Buddhist and pre-Buddhist religions in India. Most of the year, the Indian monks (and a few nuns) wandered as mendicants, but when the rains came, they gathered at centers to renew their vows and deepen their understanding. In Japan today the cycle of practice is still keyed to the seasons, with sesshins embedded in longer training periods — which in turn alternate with intervals that include only maintenance work around the monastery and light training.

Lay Zen centers in the West follow this rhythm of practice in a general way. In the Diamond Sangha, for example, we have two training periods per year, each with a seven-day and a five-day sesshin. Between training periods the practice is less demanding, though we have frequent weekend sesshins. In addition, the special eight-day Rōhatsu Ō-zesshin (Eight-Day Sesshin during Great Cold), from the evening of November 30 to the morning of December 8, is an extended celebration of the enlightenment of the Buddha Shākyamuni.

At the sesshins of most Zen Buddhist centers, students rise at 4:00 A.M. and practice zazen for twenty-five- to thirty-five-minute periods throughout the day until lights-out at 9:00 P.M. This routine is broken by intervals of formal walking between the periods of zazen, and by formal meals, a sutra service, three personal interviews each day, a talk by the Rōshi (old teacher), and brief periods of rest. Cooking, cleaning, and leadership tasks are handled by the students themselves. There is no incidental talking and the only socializing is that which one feels in the intimate circumstances of living and working together with sisters and brothers in silent, common purpose.

Zazen is, briefly, the practice of sitting erect on cushions, on a low bench, or in a chair.* The posture is such that it can be forgotten while the student devotes all possible energy to focused inquiry. For the most part, this practice is keyed to the breaths and can be the practice of counting them from one to ten, of shikantaza (sitting with no theme), or of kōan study, beginning with the word "Mu," lifted from the well-known Zen story:

> A monk asked Chao-chou, "Has the dog Buddha-nature,
> or not?"
> Chao-chou said, "Mu."†

---

* Robert Aitken, *Taking the Path of Zen* (San Francisco: North Point Press, 1982), and Yasutani Haku'un, "Introductory Lectures on Zen Training," in Philip Kapleau, *The Three Pillars of Zen: Teaching, Practice, and Enlightenment* (Boston: Beacon Press, 1965).

† Syllabus, *Wu-men kuan*, Case I; Robert Aitken, *The Gateless Barrier: The Wu-men kuan (Mumonkan)* (San Francisco: North Point Press, 1990), pp. 7–18.

"Mu" means "no" or "does not have," so the student faces a dilemma: Buddhist literature declares that all beings have Buddha-nature, yet here is perhaps the greatest Chinese master saying that the dog does not. But practice with Mu is not a matter of puzzling over this dilemma. Instead, the student sets logic aside, and musters body and mind to breathe Mu, just Mu. It is a practice that has, down through the centuries, brought countless monks, nuns, laymen, and laywomen to a realization of true nature. This is a perennial religious path and is marked with natural episodes of discouragement and despair. Many of the words in this first section are intended to encourage an inquiry into Mu in such difficult circumstances.

My custom is to appear in the dōjō during the mid-morning block of zazen to sit with the students, just before the first interviews of the day. I find something brief to say during that time, when the students are getting settled in for a period of zazen. I also come to the dōjō at the very end of the day, after the evening dokusan is over, to join the students for the closing ceremony. As the students stand before the very end, I again offer a few words. Thus, some of the "Words in the Dōjō" in this collection were originally intended to help people find their way while they were on their cushions, and some were intended for them to take along to bed.

I have arranged my pieces to reflect the various aspects of Zen practice, and added some comments. I removed the more distracting references to time and place but have left in the natural allusions. Doves, cardinals, and thrushes sing, and geckos shout at the Koko An Zendō in suburban Honolulu. Bluebirds sing and turkeys gobble at the Ring of Bone Zendō in the Sierra foothills in California. Kookaburras create their diversions at Sydney and Perth. At a sesshin in Adelaide we were serenaded by bullfrogs, and the little stream by the old Maui Zendō murmured its constant instruction. Zazen is not sensory deprivation — anything but! Birds and geckos and bullfrogs guide us. Be open to these natural teachers, wherever you may be practicing.

The First Night

Students gather for sesshin in the late afternoon the day before sesshin formally begins. They unpack, make their beds, and assemble for a work meeting. After a circle of self-introductions, sesshin jobs are assigned and explained. Newcomers are given orientation to mealtime procedures and a supper follows. At 7:00 P.M. there is one period of zazen, followed by opening remarks from the Rōshi. Dōjō leaders summarize the sesshin procedures, there is a brief period of zazen and a short sutra, and at 9:00 the students retire.

We begin our sesshin tomorrow morning at four o'clock, and continue for seven days. It is like a dream, one that is repeated each month, and is repeated elsewhere as people gather for sesshin in many places and on many occasions. We sit in this dream with students from all over the world. It is a dream of the other as no other than myself, of all time as this time now, of every place as this very Bodhi seat. The whole universe musters itself and concentrates together in sesshin — the birds, the rain, the cicadas. The circumstances are ideal. All the sesshin arrangements are settled. Everything is settled. You can forget your ordinary concerns.

I was reflecting as I unpacked my suitcase this evening that all of us bring baggage to sesshin. I want to unpack all of my baggage and put it away, and I urge you to put away your stuff too. When you forget yourself and are united with your task, that is your liberation. If there is a milestone of realization on the path, well and good, but it is in the continued practice of uniting with your work that you turn the wheel of the Dharma for yourself, for the Sangha, and for the world. As Dōgen Zenji said, "Zazen is itself enlightenment." [1]

Someone asked me, "What attitude should I hold in zazen?" I replied, "a naive attitude." If you feel comfortable and compatible with your teacher and your Sangha, then the time has come just to do it.

At the outset of each sesshin, Yasutani Haku'un Rōshi used to announce the three rules of sesshin: no talking, no looking around, and no social greetings. These rules are grounded in the complete silence of the mind, where there is full and complete communication with all sisters and brothers. Practice your Mu there, in that pure harmony.

The word "sesshin" is an ambiguous term with three intimately related meanings: "to touch the mind, to receive the mind, to convey the mind."

To touch the mind is to touch that which is not born and does not die; it does not come or go, and is always at rest. It is infinite emptiness — empty infinity — the vast and fathomless Dharma which you have vowed to understand.

To receive the mind is to be open with all your senses to instruction. Someone coughs, a window squeaks, a gecko cries, cars on the freeway hum in the distance, the bell rings, the clappers go *crack!* — these are instructive expressions of the mind, as the sound of a stone striking a stalk of bamboo instructed Hsiang-yen.[2]

Finally, you convey the mind by the utmost integrity which you present in your manner, as you stand, sit, eat, and lie down with settled dignity, composure, and recollection — as the Buddha himself or herself. You are the teacher of us all and of yourself.

You also convey the mind by containing your actions. In this way you will not distract yourself or others, and you will offer space for everyone to evolve. When I was in Japanese monasteries, I noticed that monks had a particular style of walking. There was almost no sound. You can apply this kind of care to opening the door, to eating, and so on. Contain yourself, contain Mu, and in this way you will convey the mind.

This work of touching, receiving, and conveying the mind is contained in the simple practice of the single word Mu, or the single point of "one," "two," "three," in your breath-counting.

We are lay disciples of the Buddha Shākyamuni. He felt that in order to meet the Tathāgata you must be a monk. But this idea is disproved by the lives of Vimalakīrti, the Layman P'ang, Dr. Daisetz T. Suzuki, and the many wise tea-women, nameless but not forgotten in Zen Buddhist history. Like those great lay people in our lineage, we are challenged to fold the intensive practice of the monk into our daily lives. In a very real sense, we have an advantage over the monks. The world is in our face all day long, and even during sesshin we know it is only a telephone call away. That call can come at any moment. Use your time.

With your important responsibilities to family, school, and employment, some of you will be part-timers, appearing and disappearing from the dōjō during these next few days. I am grateful that you lend your energy to our sesshin as much as you can. Please come and go as discreetly and mindfully as possible. You can find that your dōjō extends to the freeway, to your office, classroom, or shop, and to your own kitchen and living room. Use your chances. Don't mistake them for distractions.

As always, I am grateful to the planners of the sesshin who gave their careful attention and their energy to making it possible. And I am grateful to the leaders and the cooks for giving up their zazen time to help make it go. Please, everyone, make the most of this sesshin. Together we can have truly productive practice.

Coming Home

*The old-fashioned word for a psychiatrist was "alienist,"
the one who treats aliens. Zen practice is rather different
from psychiatry, but its purpose is the same. The alien
suffers from* duhkha, *the anguish of feeling displaced, and,
as the Buddha said,* duhkha *is everywhere.*[3] *It is the disease we have in common.*

Zazen seems difficult at first, for you are making yourself do it.
Take heart. It will find its own hands and feet.

Shaku Sōen Zenji said, "Zazen is not a difficult task. It is a way
to lead you to your long-lost home."[4] Some of you come from
far away, but you have joined us as though you were coming
home. You have given up important study time, career time,
family time, and recreation time to make this dōjō your life-
center for the days you are here.

We sit with the Buddha Shākyamuni beneath his tree, with his
succeeding teachers, and with all those who devoted themselves to
the Buddha Dharma. This is his dōjō, and you know that "dōjō"
is a translation of "Bodhimanda," the spot or place of enlightenment beneath the tree. Each of our cushions is the Bodhimanda.
Each of our bodies is the Bodhimanda.

You and I have taken an ordinary room and with people from all
over we have established a Zen center, a dōjō.[5] It remains for you
to make your own seat a dōjō, your own body the place of
enlightenment.

Walking from the cottage to the dōjō through the very light rain,
I reflected how the Hawaiian people regard rain as a blessing.
Then hearing the dedication of our sutra to the guardians of the

Dharma and the protectors of our sacred hall, I reflected that while there are indeed unseen guardians and protectors, the rain is also our guardian, the wind in the Bodhi leaves and Sangha members too. In this protected place settle comfortably into your practice.

In sesshin, you touch the mind — that is, you touch the place where there is no coming and going. In a very real sense, Zen Buddhist practice has no progression. This breath-moment does not come from anywhere and it has no tail of association. It is the Koko An temple, the "temple right here." You are Koko An, the temple right here. Settle into your breath-counting practice, settle into Mu, right here.

Someone asked me, "What is the most important matter?" I answered, "Intimacy." Intimacy is a step closer to the heart of things than Zen Buddhism itself. What is Zen, after all? It is just a word to describe coming home. Come home with your Mu, and you can forget about Zen.

Tung-shan wrote:

> *Everyone longs to leave the eternal flux,*
> *not just to live in harmony,*
> *but to return and sit by the charcoal fire.*[6]

Everyone longs to return home and find warmth and renewal. When the dove calls, return to Mu and sit there. Mu is not just one option among many which you select. Let all the options go, and sink into Mu. Make it your home, more and more intimately.

Completing the first day is a good reminder of how important it is to complete each period of zazen, each moment of zazen. Forget about time. Slow down and stop altogether. Stop on your

I have been reflecting on the implications of intimacy. One is gentleness with yourself and with others. Another is openness to yourself and to others. Still another is openness to your practice — to yourself practicing.

A popular teacher of meditation has declared that you must be responsible for your own practice. I understand her to mean that practice is a matter of being responsive. The many things that happen on your cushions are your teachers and guides. The Morning Star was the teacher of the Buddha. Readiness is all.

Hui-hai said, "The gate to the Dharma is relinquishment."[11] Give yourself over to breathing Mu. There is just a tiny step from distraction to attention. Take that step again and again. Maintain that step. Let yourself be reminded by the cardinal, the persistent prompting of the cardinal [a cardinal sings outside] — "Mu" — [the cardinal sings again] — "Mu" — [the cardinal sings again] — "Mu."

The old teachers have said, "You are born alone, you practice alone, and you die alone," and yet the whole universe groans and travails together, all seeking true nature. Sitting there, breathing Mu, you are breathing Mu with bushes and grasses. Settle into this universal practice.

Emptiness

The term "emptiness," in the Buddhist context, can be a problem for new students. It does not mean vacuum, but rather it is the void that is full of potential. It has no bounds.

At the first sesshin I attended in Japan, I was introduced to the monk who was to be a big brother for me during the seven days. He said, "How do you do? The world is very

ground of enlightenment, your zafu and pad, your moment. Stop with this Mu. Stop with this breath.

As lay people we cannot attend sesshin frequently, so we are challenged to treat it not merely as a periodic, intensive interval, but rather to make this the only sesshin, this moment the only moment.

The day has ended in a great wind storm and I am reminded that in the middle of the storm there is someone who is always at rest. With thoughts continually appearing and disappearing, there is someone who is never astray, who does not move. Make friends with that one, and find her ground, his ground. It is the place of the Tao, the dōjō of Mu.

The World Does Zazen

The student of Zen Buddhism finds the light of inspiration in beings and incidents of the world. Thus, unlike the way of most meditative traditions, the light is not sought exclusively within. Fundamentally, however, inside and outside are not two.

Zazen is not a practice of isolation. It is not a sensory deprivation chamber. Speculation, planning, remembering, and fantasizing — these are the things that deprive you as you sit there on your cushions.

We celebrate the great enlightenment of the Buddha Shākyamuni in this sesshin and realize that all beings are the Tathāgatha and depend upon each other. This is called mutual interdependence or dependent arising; for our purposes it means that each of us is a teacher supporting everyone else, and each of us is a student, being supported by everyone else. Let's celebrate in this spirit.

You are not alone, and your practice is not just one-to-one with a teacher. Breathe Mu and the whole world breathes Mu. Allow it to breathe Mu.

The sound of the wind and the songs of birds are essential elements of zazen, just as essential as correct posture. When the sounds die down, the silence takes their place. But if sounds and silence are missing, then you are lost in thoughts and your practice is stalling. Let sounds and silence sustain you as you face your kōan.

I am frequently asked about "great doubt." [7] There are many kinds of "great doubt." For some it is like a red-hot iron ball that cannot be vomited out. For some it is the tree breathing Mu, the bedrock-outcropping maintaining Mu, the turkeys shouting Mu. Cultivate your own great doubt by breathing Mu.

You have learned that your body sustains your zazen, so you can forget about your body. Forgetting about your body means becoming one with Mu. This practice is not limited by your skin. Truly, "Buddha nature pervades the whole universe." [8]

For a long time, Zen practice consists of noticing that you are thinking something and returning to your Mu, checking and returning, checking and returning. When you are thinking something, you are cut off. You don't hear anything. But there is another phase. When you remember to breathe Mu, you find that you are not alone, and your practice is far more than dealing with wayward thoughts. The whole room breathes Mu, the dove and mynah call Mu, the wind rustles the leaves of the Bodhi tree as Mu. Taking yourself in hand to breathe Mu, the universe is involved. This is the treasure of Zen practice.

When Hakuin Zenji said that this very place is the Lotus Land and this very body is the Buddha, he was speaking about intimacy, the imperative of our practice. "This very place is the Lotus Land" means you are intimate with the vermilion and yellow and green of the heliconia on the altar. "This very body, the Buddha" means you are truly intimate with yourself. [9] When the Buddha said, "Above the heavens, below the heavens, only I, alone and sacred," [10] he was truly intimate. Become intimate with your practice.

Like the call of the dove, each point in your breath-counting sequence, each Mu, is even closer than your hands and feet.

An incident can be instructive or disruptive, depending largely on the attitude we bring to it. If you are walking through a familiar room in complete darkness, you might bump into a table or a chair. With one kind of attitude you curse. With another you say, "Oh, there's the table — there's the chair — now I know the way." The song of the thrush and the cry of the gecko — the sounds of people coming in or going out — these can be instructive or disruptive, depending on how open you are to guidance. I hope you can respond, "Oh, now I know the way."

The world of hard definitions is not the world of zazen. The dove calls Mu and the wind blows Mu. How do you slip this dream? When you focus altogether on Mu, your senses naturally open and you find yourself in the fundamental harmony.

Why is it that the sound of the crickets goes right through? Why is it the song of the bluebird goes right through? Why feel more and more intimate with Mu? Because it really is. This is what liberates you.

---

*broad, don't you think?" I was quite charmed, but I had
no idea what he meant. Yet, as Nan-ch'üan said to Chao-
chou, "If you truly reach the genuine Tao, you will find
it as vast and boundless as outer space."*[12]

Dōgen Zenji described realization as the "body and mind dropped
away."[13] Yamada Rōshi called it "forgetting the self." Sesshin is a
time when you practice this forgetting for a few days. You don't
know if it is the second day or the fourth day, unless you are
reminded. You hear the bells that end the period of zazen, and
think, "Why! I just sat down!" Each moment is full and complete
— the empty universe itself completely in focus — simply as Mu.
This is the occasion of great promise.

Notice the little things that prevent you from forgetting yourself.
They all of them relate to yourself — "How I was, how I am, how
I will be." When you let these little things go by, you find yourself
in vastness that is also homey intimacy with Mu.

The sesshin mind is the empty mind that is always at rest. You
don't find this mind by turning yourself to it and trying to
concentrate upon it. That only makes it an abstraction. Focus on
the single word Mu. It is with the tiny specific that the empty,
silent mind is exposed.

"All things pass quickly away,"[14] indeed. Not to worry. Settle on
Mu and that will be the broadest possible space where there is no
coming into being and no going out of being. Our context is not
time. Our context is shūnyatā, the great empty sky.

As the tea-woman said to Te-shan, "Past mind cannot be grasped,
present mind cannot be grasped, future mind cannot be
grasped."[15] Mu is not a matter of the past, present, or future.
Counting the days serves only a superficial purpose. It is more

important to consider that this moment is the time of full and complete zazen.

Why should you want to cling to things of the past, the present, or the future? It is because there isn't anything else. Emptiness, the void, yawns beneath the structure, so it is natural that you should hold fast to the forms of time. The way to let go is with Mu. Cling to Mu — sink into the empty place, only with Mu. That is the way to true freedom. Everything disappears when you find yourself riding on Mu or on one, two, three. You find there is nothing there — only Mu, only one, two, three. Take that risk.

Zazen is very difficult when you try to concentrate on Mu in the context of contending thoughts. In that realm, Mu seems just one option among many. It seems very limited in the presence of so many other engaging possibilities. Please don't make it hard for yourself in this way. Listen to the silence. Breathe Mu there. Persevere and you will find it is the only option — not limited at all, but including everything.

Buddha nature pervades the whole universe inside and outside. Moreover, inside and outside are not two dimensions. This is your dōjō. This is peace. Breath-counting or Mu — your practice is peaceful. Breathe Mu. Let everything else go.

We have been studying the meaning of the "Emmei Jikku Kannon Gyō,"[16] and pertinent for us now is "Namu Butsu." This means "Veneration to the Buddha" or "Obeisance before the Buddha." It does not mean that I bow *to* a person or an image, but rather, in the presence of the Buddha I throw everything away. What is the presence of the Buddha? It is the presence of nothing at all. Please practice in that open place, that vacant place, so that there is only Mu in the whole universe, and everything else in your mind is quiet.

———

Time passes very swiftly. Yet time is an abstraction. What is not abstract? The bark of the dog, the crack of the han, the deep sound of the bell, the cry of the gecko. Blessed sounds! Let them prompt you.

Each evening we read, in Hakuin Zenji's "Song of Zazen," "Boundless and free is the sky of samādhi," and as you know, samādhi really means "one with the whole universe." Probably some of you have experienced this. At such a time, where is Mu?

Condition

> I hope you will not be preoccupied with difficulties. Thirty-five years ago, I was involved in therapy, and one day the therapist asked me, "Why did you want to catch a cold?" This made me angry, and now I think that my anger was justified. I am ready to accept the fact that I placed myself here on purpose, and that I created my condition on purpose, but I am not ready to explore in detail all the minute reasons. I hope you will agree with me. You can practice in whatever condition you find yourself, healthy or sick, happy or sad.

Everybody is in a particular condition at each moment. Female, male, old, young — some are sitting in full lotus, some are in half-lotus, some are using a bench or chair. Some are distracted by thoughts. Some are tired or angry. Legs and back can hurt from extended sitting, long-hidden worries and doubts can appear, and the difficulty of staying quiet and focused can be quite daunting. How to handle condition is one of the most difficult questions that can arise in zazen.

———

This is the first or second sesshin for quite a number of you, and I know you are suffering a lot of pain. There are several things I want to say about this matter. The first is: the purpose of sesshin is not to turn out crippled samurai. If you reach a certain point of pain, then you should sit on a bench or in a chair. If you were born lazy, I would say to you, "Sit through your pain," but I know you are not lazy. There are chairs in the alcove. Please use them. Sit there for one block of zazen and then, if you wish, return to your cushion for the next block. Or sit there for the rest of sesshin. I sat my first several sesshins in a chair — from beginning to end. You will not find quite the measure of stability on a bench or in a chair that you might find on cushions, but there is a trade-off. Even in a chair you can touch the mind. Don't let pride get in your way.

Sometimes you might find that you are creating pain by avoiding it. If you try to lift yourself somehow to avoid the pain in your knees or ankles, you create tension that makes the pain much worse. When you settle into the pain, you can actually settle through it and the pain can disappear. Tomorrow, maybe you will get your second wind and will be able to relax naturally, and then the pain will go away.

You are always in a certain condition, sometimes healthy, sometimes toxic, sometimes refreshed, sometimes stale, sometimes comfortable, sometimes uncomfortable. You are always indoors, so to speak. You may be in a palace with tapestries and picture windows, or you may be in a prison. But even in prison you can practice. Ram Dass inspired a program of meditation for prisoners and called it "The Prison Ashram Project." You are your own ashram. Practice there.

In your zazen, you might encounter a feeling of unusual sensitivity or of unusual transparency. Or you might experience fear. Walk right through these conditions. They can be very promising, but not if you focus on them.

From now on in this sesshin please forget about whether you are deep or shallow, quiet or busy — and focus only on the single point of Mu. Your condition is the context of your practice, the valley in which you follow the path. The path is your practice, not the valley.

Please don't try to breathe in a particular way. When you have deep breaths, breathe deeply. When you have shallow breaths, breathe lightly. Actually in deep zazen your breath is likely to be very light indeed. Let that condition come and go as it will. If you find you are deeply concentrated and hardly breathing at all, then at such a time, lightly cut the link between your breath and Mu, and just sit there motionless, facing Mu with all your resolute spirit.

Today has been a tired day and tomorrow you may be tired too. This is all right. As Yasutani Rōshi used to say, "When you are tired, the enemy is tired." When you are tired, Mu is tired. When you nod, come back to Mu. In your tired condition, you are free of "certain certainties" and can enter easily into the mythic, dreamlike dimension where zazen is most effective. If you try to wake yourself up, you might be successful for thirty seconds, but then you will slip back to the natural state of your body at the time. Maintain your zazen in that sleepy condition. You are no longer remembering, scheming, or fantasizing. Dream-thoughts and dream-images come and go. When you nod, come back to Mu. That is true zazen.

I can see that the enemy is getting tired. Buck up. Perhaps tomorrow both of you can give over.

I am always saying that zazen is a zigzag path. But don't let yourself be managed by your swings of mood. Remember how it was when your zazen was comfortable and Mu was steady and easy. Remembering that pleasant condition, you are in that pleasant condition. Settle into Mu there. Pursue Mu there.

By now each of you has experienced intervals of intimacy, of harmony. It is instructive to notice when these intervals come. They come when you focus only on Mu, only on breath-counting, only on a kōan. Settle into Mu, let everything else go.

It is hot this sesshin — a difficult condition in which to do zazen. Don't suppose that such a difficult condition is an adversary that you must overcome with your practice. Your condition is yourself. You practice as your condition.

> A monk asked Tung-shan, "When heat and cold visit us, how should we avoid them?"
>
> Tung-shan said, "Why not go where there is neither heat nor cold?"
>
> The monk said, "Where is there neither heat nor cold?"
>
> Tung-shan said, "When it is hot, let the heat kill you. When it is cold, let the cold kill you."[17]

Heat is the field of your practice, just as sometimes anger is the field of your practice, or peace, or sadness, or importunate thoughts. But if you give attention to the field, you are neglecting your work. Our model is Fudō, sitting there on our altar. In sculpture or in painting he is often sitting in the flames of Hell. His name means "Immovable," but he is moving — he is breathing in and out. Breathe in and out with your practice. When you are aware of your breathing, there are no thoughts.

Thoughts come and go without ceasing, it seems. But listen to the silence. Are there any thoughts there?

Take advantage of your condition. Use your condition. If you feel strange or weird, don't try to recover your common state of mind. Go straight along with Mu in that strange, weird condition. It can be very promising. Breathe Mu, only Mu.

Preoccupation with condition is the bête noire of Zen, the black beast of practice, the bugaboo of true zazen. Don't give that animal a second glance or it will eat you up and take over. Let your condition go, let everything go and simply face your kōan.

"Body and mind dropped away" is an experience, and the way to that experience is to let body and mind subside. Let them subside with Mu. Let Mu be the subsided body and mind.

Your purpose is not to attain a certain mental or emotional state. Even "purpose" is not a suitable word. Your function is to breathe Mu, to let Mu breathe Mu. Everything arises from this. Everything arises *with* this.

Thoughts of condition can be troublesome. Of course if you have the flu or a pinched nerve, you must lie down. If there's a fire, you must gather up Bodhidharma and go outside. But there is a vast range of conditions, inner and outer, that you can ignore. Katsuki Sekida told us a story that was current just after the great earthquake in 1922 in which much of Tokyo was destroyed. An operation was in progress in a hospital. The doctor and staff carried it forward and completed it even though the lights went out and they were dependent on natural lighting from the windows. The electrical system failed too, and the building rocked violently. It was only when the patient had been wheeled out that they looked at each other and said, "That was an earthquake."

Sometimes you are clear and sometimes you are foggy. Sometimes you are quiet and sometimes you are noisy. Perhaps you are consistently foggy and noisy. If so, walk there with Mu. Nothing is static. The fog clears, the chatter dies down. But if you judge yourself foggy or noisy, you are setting up temporary impediments. Breathe Mu as best you can. Angels can do no more.

It is natural to wonder, "How am I doing?" Let me reassure you. You're doing fine. But please don't linger in evaluation. It can be a big distraction. Settle in the place of no stages with your Mu.

The Single Point

> During a sesshin in Japan, the Rōshi will commonly speak
> about the development of the sesshin. Often, he will use the
> metaphor of a battle. He might say, "Now we are preparing
> for battle," or "Now we are drawing up our battle lines,"
> or "Now we are meeting the enemy." It is not false to
> think of sesshin as development or confrontation. But there
> is another way. There is no time at all. No development,
> no ongoing practice. There is only this thought-moment,
> only this Mu-moment.

As Wu-men said, you must devote yourselves to the single point of the word Mu.[18] Penetrate the tip of a hair, and everything changes — "a single spark lights your Dharma candle."[19]

One day is enough. One moment is enough. Each moment is plenty of time. Each moment, each thought-frame, each Mu is full and complete. Why is that? It has no dimensions. So then what is Mu? Don't say it is nothing.

Actually, the expression "plenty of time" means no time at all. Enter there, practice there. In that silence beneath the Bodhi tree, where is time? The point of Mu is the meaningful point of no dimension. Lost in that profound dream, you are truly settled in your practice.

We probably measure time by the incidence of our thoughts. When there are no thoughts, there is no time. Key Mu to your breath. Let your Mu be breathy. In this way, there will be no room for thoughts and your Mu will be infinitely spacious.

Someone asked me, "How long will it take me?" I said, "No time at all."

In true zazen, or I may say, in ordinary zazen, there are no dimensions. There is no time at all and also no space: the drum and the bell sound in our hearts. The gecko calls from the very center of the mind. "Buddha nature pervades the whole universe, existing right here and now."[20]

The Buddha Shākyamuni is our model. Seated in silence he is in the dimension of no coming or going. He shows us that eternity is not a matter of endless future. It is this moment. Practice the Buddha there. Face your kōan there.

Whether you have been living at the Zendō or have come from your home nearby, or from far away, you have naturally been caught up in the momentum of your everyday life. A preoccupation with your daily affairs will tend to continue as you sit there on your cushions. Please slow down. Your best zazen will come when you are completely settled into this breath-moment. When you focus upon the point, then you are giving the point a chance to clarify itself. When you are completely settled and your Mu is completely motionless, then you find there is nothing before or after, only this breath, only this Mu. That's it!

Carry Your Practice Lightly

When I first started zazen in earnest, I was in Japan. I felt isolated, and I worried about my personal problems and my inability to communicate. Then when I turned my attention to Mu, I was pretty grim about it. One day, my teacher Nakagawa Sōen Rōshi listened to my presentation in dokusan, and said, "Please carry your Mu lightly."

"How can I do that?" I wondered.

You and I have a monitor upstairs, a voice that reminds us to stay on the beam. Without such a monitor, we cannot do zazen, but too many reminders make us dwell on our weaknesses. When the monitor becomes a judge, throw him out, throw her out.

Your conscience is your consciousness, the sense you have in common with all beings. It shows you clearly what is right and what is wrong, what is appropriate and what is not. Some people, however, grow up without a sense that they are members of the great family. They create all kinds of trouble for themselves and others. Be glad you have a conscience! Yet it is possible to give conscience too much control, as though it were a parent dealing with a small child. Allow your conscience its appropriate role, and it will be your cogent teacher.

Sōen Rōshi used to say that sesshin is a symphony. At the end he would play a recording of the fourth movement of Beethoven's Ninth by way of celebration. There are many parts and movements and intervals in our sesshin symphony. Together we re-create Shākyamuni's composition. Individually we find fulfillment in our parts. Enjoy your playing. Enjoy your practice.

———

By now some of you may feel that Mu is a heavy burden. But, you know, Yamada Rōshi said, "To tell the truth, Mu has no meaning." Where could there be any weight? Carry Mu lightly, and all your other concerns will be light as well. Lighten up and Mu will become clear.

I am prompted to recall Thich Nhat Hanh's words that Buddhism is not a battlefield. Indeed the human heart is not a battlefield. The world is not a battlefield. You are not seeking to master Mu, or to penetrate Mu, but rather to admit Mu.

Perhaps you have a tendency to treat zazen quite grimly, especially during sesshin. But really it is a very interesting practice, with your strengths, your weaknesses, your physical qualities, your mental and emotional qualities — all of them at play. You seek intimacy with Mu. What an interesting challenge it is! Pursue that challenge with childlike enthusiasm, like a scientist. Regard the whole process objectively, knowing that your best is also the Buddha's best.

If you are grim about your Mu, then it will form a kind of heavy continuity, a hard shell, and there will be no place for the cicadas or the kookaburra to penetrate. When Chao-chou said "Mu," he was a tottering old priest and probably he said it very softly. This is a clue to how we should hold our Mu. With determination, of course, but the Mu itself is very soft. Essential nature itself is very soft. In fact, it has no substance at all.

"Great doubt" is passion for practice and a dynamic unity of Mu with body and mind. But there are little doubts and these can be impediments. You might be checking yourself with the questions, "How am I doing? What is happening to me? Am I doing it right?" However natural such questions might be, they are quite distracting. Yamada Rōshi used to say, "The practice of Zen is forgetting the self in the act of uniting with something." During sesshin, that something is your practice. Forget yourself completely in your intimacy with your practice. Stay with Mu there and let unfold what will unfold.

When you judge your practice as deep or shallow, clear or confused, you are dividing yourself from Mu. Your eye is on condition, and so you deviate. Please trust the process. Breathe Mu. Settle into Mu. Let Mu breathe Mu.

You all know about returning to Mu when your mind strays, but often it is your mood that prompts your mind to stray. You can remind yourself to return to Mu, but if your mood doesn't change, then you will quickly stray again. Usually it is something gloomy, so please reflect that a hundred years from now it won't make any difference. Ask yourself, "Who am I to take myself so seriously?" When your mood breaks up, you can return to Mu easily and freely, and be comfortable in your work there.

Smile at yourself and at your humanity. The Buddha himself was visited by dancing maidens and sundry other temptations. You partake of the nature of the Buddha Shākyamuni, and so you tend to have many thoughts and feelings. Treat this tendency gently and take up Mu again with good humor.

Zazen is a matter of coping with mistakes, but it is not the way of self-blame. Extend loving kindness to yourself. Be easy on yourself. It can be useful to acknowledge your feelings of guilt, but set them to one side right away with the thought, "I'll talk to you guys after sesshin." Then settle into Mu, settle into your practice, and let all your feelings go.

Zazen is not an adversarial practice. It is the way to give yourself a chance. When you give yourself a chance, you enjoy hearing — you enjoy Mu. Finding this enjoyment is an important milestone.

Enjoy the air, the warmth, your body, and your ⌐
traveler enjoys the sky.

Attention

*How gratifying it is to sit in the dokusan room and have
someone come and exclaim in a smile, "The tape in my
head has switched off!" Attention to the point has brought
this happy condition into being. Now attention can nurture
the point and let it flower.*

Yasutani Rōshi said, "When you do zazen, your eyes do zazen."
With your eyelids lowered, you nonetheless look straight ahead,
concentrating rigorously on Mu. Attention!

Attention is the essence of our practice, the teaching of all our
ancestors. Incomplete attention is diffused and from there you
wander into your old cycles of preoccupation. Come back to your
sharp attention. This is the way of intimacy. Without attention
there can be no intimacy.

It is very easy and natural to maintain the Way. When you are
thinking something, only a tiny shift of attention will bring you
back to Mu or to the first point of your breath-counting sequence.
Tiny as it is, don't neglect it. When you notice that you are
straying: Mu.

Attention is more than a matter of focusing. It is completion.
Where you are not attentive, everything is a blur. When you are
attentive, each thing stands out like a bell sounding in the silence
— each Mu, each breath, each act. So whether you are opening a
door or doing Mu on your cushions, let your act stand forth. Let

each inhalation be altogether itself, each exhalation altogether itself, each Mu altogether itself.

Continuous attention to Mu is very difficult, and perhaps impossible. Complete your attention to Mu at the end of each breath. Hold your mind still and quiet as you inhale, and then exhale Mu as though for the first time, fresh and new. Make a practice of finishing each Mu. With the first breath — Mu. With the next breath — Mu. Bring each breath, each thought frame, each Mu to a close.

Attention does not require being wide awake. Please devote yourself to Mu even when you are feeling dreamy. In fact maybe it is better then. Give your full attention to Mu, whatever your condition. Dreaminess can be a distraction, but so are your thoughts about how cleverly you can respond in the dokusan room. The chances are that such thoughts don't appear when you are dreamy. Only the most random kind of images appear and disappear. Count your blessings. Practice where you are.

I have been thinking about the word "concentration," a word I don't use very much. It implies two things — the one who concentrates and the thing concentrated upon. Simone Weil remarks that when she tells her students to concentrate, they don't concentrate; they just tense their muscles.[21] Investment is a better word. Invest yourself in Mu. Devote yourself to Mu.

You might find that one problem in your practice is an anxiety to get on with it. You dwell upon time, and so your attention is diffused and your Mu is just a blur. Please resist this tendency. Make your Mu an interlude. Make your next Mu an interlude. Configure each Mu, each breath moment.

One reason we celebrate the Buddha and his successors is that they did not get caught up in byways.

A monk asked Chao-chou, "What is the path?"
Chao-chou said, "It runs along inside the fence."
The monk said, "I'm not asking about that path."
Chao-chou said, "What path are you asking about?"
The monk said, "The great path."
Chao-chou said, "The great path leads to the capital." [22]

Straight ahead!

It occurs to me that some people might slow up their practice by thinking "I want realization for myself." Zazen is like all other human pursuits in its requirement that you forget your self in the practice — in devotion to your task. If you have attainment foremost in your mind, then whatever your endeavor, you will end up being unnatural and awkward. Try being more impersonal. Attention is your instrument. Use your instrument of attention to its fullest capacity and let your organism settle into Mu — sink into Mu. Forget everything else.

When your sesshin has matured, you might feel, "Oh, my zazen is pretty good," but remember what it is that has kept the Buddha Dharma a living stream down through the centuries — the spirit of "Not yet, not enough, not enough yet." Realization takes only a moment, but it requires diligent attention to come upon that moment. There is only one requisite: remember to practice. Remembering to practice is Right Recollection. But this is not a matter of moving from one thing to another. In this very moment, only Mu — Mu.

Each night we recite the "Song of Zazen" by Hakuin Zenji. It includes the message that the practice of reciting the name of the Buddha, the practice of repentance, the practice of the perfections — the Pāramitās — all have their source in zazen. Where does zazen have its source? In attention. Attention — that is the Tao.

Coming and Going

In Far Eastern languages, many idioms link "coming" with "going." The polite way to bid good-bye to your household is to say, "I go and return." Coming and going, we are near or far, old or young, dying or being born, here in this "floating world." Yet the floating world can also be rooted, as we learn when we settle ourselves in zazen and then stand for the next ceremony.

Midway during sesshin it is good to reflect that we are always in the middle day, the middle hour, the middle moment. But in fact that middle moment does not exist. It is only conceptual. Never mind about concepts. Where is Mu?

In this sesshin, as the earth turns, the flame trees bloom and summer begins. Let yourself turn with the earth, breath by breath, rooted in Mu.

With his enlightenment, the Buddha said, "Now I see that all beings are the Tathāgata. Only their delusions and preoccupations keep them from testifying to the fact." [23]

All beings are the Buddha, but they have not yet evolved to the point where they can acknowledge it. They are clinging to preoccupations. What preoccupations? I think preoccupations are feelings that something is missing. A home, perhaps, or a spouse, or a family, or a career. These are important elements of human fulfillment, but fixation upon them certainly can get in the way. The Buddha encouraged his students to leave home, to forget about family, to forget about career, and to devote themselves solely to the process of transformation that brings great enlightenment and great peace. But we as lay people cannot let these things go. They are essential to our lives. So the question becomes, How do I leave home without leaving home? The answer is right here in this sesshin. As important as home and family and job can be for us, it is essential that we let our preoccupations with these things go, completely. It turns out that we forget them just for a moment, but the act of forgetting is complete during that short interval. The Buddha's own experience was momentary. Afterwards he returned to his disciples, altogether fresh and new. Afterwards we return to our responsibilities, altogether fresh and new.

When sesshin is over, there is always the question, How shall I maintain the silence of zazen in daily life? Well, your practice of such maintenance begins now. Going up the stairs, using the bathroom, taking off your clothes, lying down to sleep — keep your mind steady and clear.

When you think only in terms of sequence, you are like the one in the midst of water crying out in thirst. When you think just in terms of future attainment you are like the child of a wealthy home wandering among the poor. Let down your bucket where you are. The water is fresh right here.

I want to speak about kinhin (the formal walk between periods of zazen). How do you hold your mind in kinhin? I count the number of steps I take with each exhalation, and then with each inhalation. I count two steps for each exhalation, two steps for each inhalation. You could try this, or you could say Mu, Mu with each exhalation, Mu, Mu with each inhalation in time with your steps. Body, mind, spirit, will are thus unified and you are doing zazen as you walk.

For some of you, this is the middle day. For others, tonight is the last night. Two-day sesshins, five-day sesshins, seven-day sesshins — all are complete sesshins. Don't become preoccupied with time. If you think in terms of sequence, you will feel there is not much time left in this sesshin, but this is not the true way. It is just your "consciousness up to now":

> Students of the way do not know truth,
> they only know their consciousness up to now;
> this is the source of endless birth and death —
> the fool calls it the original self. [24]

With the storm coming and going — with noise before and peace now, you can appreciate Hakuin's words about coming and going, never astray.

Each beat of the drum, each clack of the han, is a thought-moment, containing the past, present, and future, and all other dimensions. But I think I stress this fact too much. I discount sequence because in your consciousness of sequence, the virtue of the single point can get obscured. Yet the sequence is a complementary virtue. When Chao-chou said "Mu," he was showing just that point, but he was also showing how to do it. Zazen is a process, moment by moment, week after week, year after year throughout our lives.

Some teachers enjoin their students to penetrate Mu, to break into Mu. This is misleading, I think. Wu-men makes it clear that in practicing Mu you engage in a process, a ripening,[25] and there are two things to be said about it. The first is that it is all right to be where you are in this process. And the second is, of course, that you enhance the ripening by breathing Mu with each breath.

The "red-hot iron ball" is the powerful, compelling sense that Mu is breathing Mu. Cultivate that Mu. Nurture your Mu. Let yourself become big with Mu.

———

Human life and indeed all life is made up of cycles — now waking, now sleeping — and for us, now sesshin, now everyday life. But Wu-men said, "Carry Mu with you day and night."²⁶ The cycles do not exclude each other, it seems. With time so precious in sesshin Wu-men's words are especially important. How do you carry Mu with you at night? Yasutani Rōshi used to say, "When you go to bed don't think, 'Now that is over with — now I can get some sleep.'" Of course you need to get your sleep, but you can make sleep your practice. Breathe Mu as you lay out your bed and take off your clothes. Lie down to sleep with Mu. Don't focus so intently that you keep yourself awake — hold Mu lightly as you lie there. Let your dream companions gather and you will drop off to sleep. Somehow your zazen will continue — your Mu will continue. It is not that your waking Mu becomes a dreaming Mu, but rather that your sesshin dream continues through the twenty-four hours. Perhaps you will wake up with Mu in the middle of the night, and then you can quietly breathe Mu as you fall asleep again. Tomorrow morning you might find Mu on your lips as you awaken. Thus you carry it, day and night.

Patience

Cheerless endurance is the ultimate kind of patience — at one end of the scale. But if your practice is bleak, then the upshot of your practice will be bleak. Zazen is not a means to an end. Means and ends are actually the same. Try cheerful patience. That's the other end of the scale.

Many people think of zazen practice as a sequential development, and on a couple of occasions recently, I have encountered the expression: "to pass Mu." I don't think I have ever used that expression but it seems to be floating around anyway. In fact, I often quote a colleague who says, "I have never passed Mu." I, too, have never passed Mu. And the people working on other kōans, too, seem caught up in sequence. "On to the next one and the next." I may be responsible for this. If so, I take it all back. It was quite a revelation to me to work with the people in Argentina who are doing kōan study. They would stop with each kōan and then, after doing well, they would come back the next time and say, "I didn't go on to the next kōan. I'd like to take up the last one again." And they would have some question. This was very heartening for me. So please let yourself linger with your kōan.

It is natural to feel impatient during sesshin. "When will I ever get it?" But patience is the Tao of all the Buddhas. Patience is not endurance. It is loving acceptance, loving acceptance, breath by breath. And when you follow the way of patience you find your own best realization, not someone else's.

Like the other Pāramitās, from the perfection of charity to the perfection of wisdom, the perfection of patience is the quality of enlightenment. With the discomforts of sesshin, we are especially aware that all life is suffering. Sickness, suffering — it is this that preoccupied the Buddha. "Why should there be suffering in the world?" But consider the etymology of the word "suffer." It can mean "to permit, to allow." In this spirit of permission, take up Mu, just Mu, and you will find no resistance at all.

In this long, leisurely sesshin you have learned to dwell nowhere in no time and so you have no need for powerful endurance. Breathe Mu there.

When you look back on the days of sesshin that have passed, you will discern many changes in yourself. Cultivate your Mu, and many new changes will come.

When you breathe each Mu as your last, your patience is transformed, and you have entered the realm of trust. There is no anxiety there. Settle into Mu with each breath, where you are, as you are. Then you are at ease, and no longer anxious. This ultimate kind of patience with yourself and with your Mu will carry you across. Give Mu your patient attention.

The Sacred Self

The self is simply a bundle of perceptions. Perceptions themselves, their organs, and things perceived are without substance, as the Heart Sutra tells us.[27] *Yet at the same time, the self is the agent of realization and the setting of serious practice.*

The Buddha pointed out that it is difficult to be born a human being and difficult then to find the Buddha Dharma. Indeed. When you reflect on the infinite number of happenstances that coalesced to produce you, then you understand how unique, how precious, how sacred you really are. Your task is to cultivate that precious, sacred nature and help it to flower.

Hakuin Zenji, and teachers who went before him and have come after, affirm that "All beings by nature are Buddha . . . This very body is the Buddha."[28] When we translate this into everyday terms, we gain the assurance: "I am all right to the very bottom." This is not merely the pop psychology of "I'm okay; you're okay" — but the realization that I am really all right from the beginning.

Thus, high ideals are held out to you as a Zen student, but not unreal ones. Shākyamuni was a human Buddha; you are a human Buddha. This is lofty enough. You can practice your rightness *as if* you really know that you are all right. You are not being a Pollyanna. The practice *as if* is the practice of taking yourself in hand and making real what has always been true.

It is the Buddha who can declare that I am all right from the beginning but I have this problem in testifying to that rightness. Step by step — breath by breath with Mu, your delusions and preoccupations drop away, and the moonlight of ages before the Buddha shines clearly.

"All right to the very bottom" means all right with all your differences and peculiarities — for these make up the individuation you seek in this multi-centered universe.

Tung-shan shows in the first of his Five Modes of Honor and Virtue that it is with an acknowledgment of your own Buddhahood and nobility that you truly begin your practice: "As the sacred master, make the way of [Emperor] Yao your own." [29] Your practice becomes living up to your own innate Buddhahood and nobility and realizing it through your Mu.

It is important not to belittle yourself when you catch yourself straying off into thinking. Please don't be perfectionistic and expect too much of yourself. The Buddha spent many long years in hard practice under the Bodhi tree before he realized something. You have a difficult time because you share his nature. Accept that sacred nature. Sink into Mu. Settle into Mu. Let everything else go.

You are always establishing your practice — during kinhin, during breakfast. Remember your kōan; remember your breath-counting. Thoughts appear but they are not separate from yourself. They are not someone else. Accept yourself, take pleasure in yourself, enjoy yourself. Do contending thoughts come? Okay, let's go back to Mu. It is like that.

Don't wait for something to correct itself. Just as you are, breathe Mu, in this breath, this breath. Settle into each moment with the confidence of the Buddha. Smile at all the conditioning that said you were not worthy.

You may feel, "Oh, I have these weaknesses and these faults and they are impeding my practice." But really faults and weaknesses are only pejorative words for qualities. Really they are points of growth, points of change. Your laziness is your patience and your anger is your sense of justice.

I reflect that the Buddha's path as he moved from practice to practice can be instructive for us on our own way. He gave up austerities, and took up the practice of zazen. It is important that we too give up being hard on ourselves, that we accept ourselves for what we are. It is the culmination of the Buddha's practice, and our own, to realize that from the beginning we are the Tathāgata. So be easy on yourself; let Mu breathe Mu.

Our practice is not an exercise in self-improvement. "The sky of samādhi and the moonlight of wisdom form the temple of our practice."[30] There is nothing blocking us. "Nirvana is right here before our eyes."[31] The Kingdom of God is at hand.

Though Shaku Sōen Zenji said, "Zazen is not a difficult task,"[32] it is nonetheless full of difficulties. Though Hakuin Zenji said, "This very body is the Buddha," still one is naturally beset by many doubts. Yet Shaku Sōen and Hakuin are right, after all.

"Our friends and family members guide us as we walk the ancient way."[33] These are not divergent ways before you. Not only do friends and family members show us the way, not only do Sangha members show us the way, but you yourself, I myself, know the way. Step forth.

Becoming Settled

Each moment is eternity itself. How do you practice that? Come to a halt. Stay there. Settle there. Treat each breath as though it were your last. Someone asked me, "How should I treat each breath as though it were my last?"

I said, "Breathe Mu. Settle into Mu. Sink into Mu. Put everything else to one side. Let everything else go. Let there be only Mu. Let Mu breathe Mu."

Some of you are experiencing bodily tension, and with your concern about making the most of your time, this is natural. Hakuin Zenji's recipe for tension was to imagine that you place a cake of oily aromatic incense on the top of your head. Let it melt down through your brain and your neck, shoulders, chest, belly, and on out to the tips of your extremities — purifying and perfuming your entire body.[34]

Tension comes when you are thinking something. Your facial muscles stiffen up, and this begins a spiral, for the more tense you are, the more intense your thinking becomes, and the less attention you can give to your practice.

Cut the string and relax your face — then relax your forehead, cheeks, chin, neck, shoulders, chest. Take a deep breath, and let your stomach hang out naturally. Settle into Mu, or into your breath-counting, and let everything else go.

Let your weight rest in your belly. Notice that sometimes you try to hold yourself erect by raising yourself from your cushions somehow. This way leads only to exhaustion. Swallow your consciousness into your lower abdomen, and let it become tender. Relax your abdomen. If you find that you have relaxed your abdomen, relax it some more, until you are breathing from the very bottom. There are no thoughts there, only Mu.

Are you hanging on? That's what makes it hard to let go. Just settle into your Mu. Kuan-yin has a nice soft tummy.

Consider for a moment that each of your exhalations, however long or short it might be, is really a sigh. Let yourself down with each exhalation, as though it were a sigh. Our grandmothers knew that when they sighed, they could let their worries go.

When you find your mind racing, take one long Mu-sigh and listen to the sounds — the wind in the trees, the squeak of the window, the songs of the birds. Then resume your normal breathing with Mu, and if your mind races again, take one long Mu-sigh again. Let the birdsong prompt you to let down. Let yourself all the way down.

You don't have to cut off your thoughts. When you are completely still, you find there are no thoughts to cut off. But when you are thinking of something, you are wavering, even physically. When you settle into the single point of Mu, then in a single breath-moment, everything disappears. There are no dimensions whatever. Breathe Mu there.

As our sesshin settles, it becomes clear why people are advised not to move when they do zazen. Essential nature is completely steady. Let yourself be a mountain of Mu. The Buddha Shākyamuni on our altar touches the ground with his right hand in a teaching mudrā, showing that he is rooted to the center of the earth. Send the roots of your practice down and sink to the bottom of the world. Root yourself like the Buddha, as the Buddha.

Settle comfortably into your practice, but keep yourself completely alert, like a cat watching a mouse-hole.

We all of us know what it is to be too speedy and we know the importance of slowing down. Let your breath slow you down. Let your breath bring you to a complete standstill. Rest there in your belly with Mu. Don't give an inch.

You often hear me say, "Sink into Mu, settle into Mu," and it may seem that the important words are "sink" and "settle." They are important, but more important is the question, "What is Mu?"

Notice how in deep zazen, everything comes to rest. In that realm, face Mu. There your practice will bloom and bear fruit.

Though I usually speak about Mu and breath-counting, I also teach *shikantaza,* pure sitting, to those who find the empty sky to be the best metaphor for their practice. If this is your way, please translate my homilies and teishōs accordingly. Thoughts come and go, feelings arise and pass away. This is the context of your pure sitting, just as it is for the student of Mu or breath-counting. You are like a shrine with no walls, no floor, and no roof. There is nothing at all there. Even peace and silence do not describe it. Steady! Steady!

Switch Back to Mu

In his workshops, Thich Nhat Hanh says, "Your mind is like a TV. When you want a busy channel, you switch to a busy channel. When you want a quiet channel, you switch to a quiet channel."

When you are thinking something, you need only to shift your attention slightly to come back to Mu, or to the first point of your breath-counting sequence. Tiny as this shift may be, don't neglect it. When you notice that you are straying off — "Mu."

———

The path of Mu is clearly marked, like a hiking trail with white painted stones. Leaves in the wind, the calling of doves, the scoldings of mynahs are your teachers. Your thoughts themselves can be reminders. Their appearance is your signal.

The mind that is open to sounds is the clear mind. The mind that is open to sounds is the clean mind. As you practice, keep yourself open to sounds, not closed off in your self. Keep yourself open to the crickets. Buddha nature pervades the whole universe. You are sitting there in the Buddha's dream, as you focus on Mu. The universe is vast and fathomless, filled with great shining light. But if you are thinking something or dwelling on your feelings, you are confined in a narrow place. Come back to the universe. Come back to your practice.

The faraway rooster is part of your natural setting. So is the sound of the stream and the whistle of the cardinal. Sit there in that natural setting. When the rooster, the stream, and the cardinal are not present in your zazen, the chances are that you are occupied with thoughts. Return to those sounds; settle there into Mu.

Tung-shan said, "Don't wander about in your head and validate shadows anymore."[35] Don't limit yourself to your brain. It is too hard to do zazen alone. If you sit there cut off from the world, you might be able to stay with Mu for three or four breaths, but then you slip away. Open yourself to the world, the sound of the wind, the airplanes overhead. Like familiar objects in the dark, they help you to stay oriented.

The practice of exacting attention in daily life will resolve many difficulties. Zazen is no different. When you notice that you are distracted, come back to your task. When you are thinking of something there on your cushions, come back to Mu. But there are other kinds of distractions besides thinking. Vagueness and diffusion also separate you from your task. When you find yourself in a vague or diffused condition, let that act of noticing be like a bell that brings you back to Mu.

Zazen itself teaches zazen. Even your tendencies to get ahead of yourself in your practice are your good teachers. Take your signal from them, and return to your center, at Mu.

You can do zazen when you are still a bit unsettled. However, when you feel that you could be more settled, make a point of taking a sigh. Breath brings life and maintains life. Breath brings purity and maintains purity. Give yourself over to your breath, and your mind will be silent. Face Mu there.

Please don't be harsh with yourself. Don't force anything. Nurture yourself and your practice. When you notice that you are thinking something, then gently and comfortably come back to your practice — back to Mu, back to your breath-counting.

Perhaps you have noticed that when you are thinking something you are enclosed in yourself, and when you are truly focused on Mu, on counting your breaths or on following your breath, you are open to everything. The sound of the rain goes right through — the sound of distant thunder — that's it!

In long sesshins, there is a certain rhythm, a certain momentum that builds up, and you might try to wear away your distractions and finally reach a quiet place toward the last day or so. In short sesshins, you don't have the luxury of time. Your only option is just to switch the distractions off. Take one long conscious breath, in and out, and notice that nothing remains. Stay there and settle into your practice.

From time to time some sort of psychological intimation may rise to the surface of your mind during your zazen. This can be very helpful in understanding yourself. In the same way, helpful thoughts about business, family, or an intellectual pursuit may occur to you. All such thoughts can be used, but they should not be cultivated during zazen. That cultivation belongs in another time and place. You cannot forget yourself if you are working on yourself. Put your thoughts to one side and settle into Mu. Sink into Mu. Let everything else go. Let there be only Mu in the whole world. Everything else in your mind is quiet.

When you focus on the single point of your practice, the doves chant Mu in your heart. The wind blows Mu through the finely tuned strings of your mind. People come and go through your skin, infinitely porous.

The scent of the night jasmine reminds you and guides you and keeps you steady as you pursue Mu.

Diligence

Zen teachers like to draw circles. Sometimes they draw them around from right to left, sometimes around from left to right. These circles can represent emptiness, fullness, or the moon. Or they can represent the practice. The circle that goes around from right to left — against the path of the sun on the sundial — represents the hard way of practice before any glimmer of understanding appears. When it goes around from left to right, following the path of the sun, it represents the easier way of practice after a glimmer opens the Way. But both before and after the glimmer, the practice requires investment and conscientious diligence.

I was reminded tonight of my old teacher Senzaki Nyogen Sensei, who told us that when he was a young monk at Engakuji he became ill with tuberculosis, and had to be isolated in a little hut.

Meals were brought to him, and once in a while his teacher, Shaku Sōen Zenji, visited. One day he said to his teacher, "What if I should die?" Shaku Sōen said, "If you die, just die." This retort changed his life completely, and he began to recover. Ultimately he was able to move from his little hut back to the monks' hall. As he was packing up, he found in the back of a drawer the medicine which he had stopped taking after that exchange with his teacher. This is not to deny the importance of medicine, but rather to stress the Great Death which is really the purpose of sesshin, as it is the purpose of all true religious practice.

Zazen is not a matter of exerting muscular energy. It is simply a matter of being truly serious. It is important for you to personalize Hakuin's assurance that this very body is the Buddha. He has set forth a grave responsibility for you.

It is natural at this time in sesshin to feel, "I have pushed as hard as I can and now I will stay in this ultimate place and wait." I honor your effort, but zazen continues to teach zazen. Watch for the hints, the clues that will help you to be even more intimate with Mu.

How can you push it even more? When you walk up the stairs, walk with Mu, as Mu. When you change clothes for the work period, "Mu." When you pick up the broom, "Mu." When you wash your hands and face afterwards, "Mu." When you breathe out — "Mu." When you breathe out again — "Mu."

Not only does time go by very quickly, but chances appear and disappear. Use your time.

Anguish is everywhere, the Buddha said. Its cause is our self-preoccupations, and their release is in our practice. Please persevere.

We have a tendency to think, "Oh, there's always next sesshin," just as in daily life we think, "There's always tomorrow." Don't bet on it. This is the last breath of the last block of sitting of the last sesshin. Tomorrow simply isn't in the contract. I was recalling as I made my bows just now that the person who made this bowing mat and this zafu died after she sent them and before they reached us by parcel post. We all of us are at risk, and the tendency to postpone is a pernicious trap. Where will you be next November or even at the time of our next sesshin? You can't say. The time of true life is this very thought-frame.

Some of you have asked me how you can control your thoughts. Who is in charge here? When you breathe in and then breathe out, are there any thoughts there? Focus scrupulously on breathing in and breathing out.

There is a certain place in your zazen where you feel comfortable and concentrated. But it isn't enough. Once I asked my teacher, Nakagawa Sōen Rōshi, "When I am in deep zazen, Mu tends to slip away, leaving me sitting there very quietly. Is this all right?" He said, "In that deep place, hold fast to Mu." In that deep place, what is Mu? Where is Mu?

It is important that you give your practice your best push. At the same time, zazen is not merely an exercise in self-improvement. You are walking the Buddha's path. Each morning you take refuge in the Buddha, the Dharma, and the Sangha:

> *Buddham saranam gacchāmi*
> *Dhammam saranam gacchāmi*
> *Sangham saranam gacchāmi*[36]

I take refuge in the Buddha, Dharma, and Sangha. I find my home there. Zazen is a religious practice in the hardest, deepest, and least sectarian sense of the word. You practice religiously.

When you begin to build a certain momentum in your sesshin, it is very important that you use this power. It is possible of course to coast on your power, but then you would not be using your sesshin well. Remember that the old worthies did not just chug along in their practice contentedly. No, their spirit was "Not yet! Not enough! Not enough yet!"

Someone asked me, "How can I persevere?" I said, "You persevere as the world perseveres." The hammering up the street perseveres as your Mu with your breath. Keep yourself open to the Mu-sounds of the world. They are your own Mu as you breathe in and out.

If you regard Zen Buddhism as a practice that will help you from outside, you cannot get the most from it. You yourself are your practice. Invest yourself in your practice.

At some point you must go beyond mere survival of sesshin difficulties. Decide what your purpose is in coming here. Formulate that as a vow. Repeat this vow when you sit down at the outset of each period. You are fulfilling your vow if you follow through, whatever happens.

This is a time when you can say, "I acknowledge my talents and my limitations. I will work diligently during this sesshin and I will make the four great Bodhisattva Vows my lifetime practice."[37]

When you first sit down, please don't allow yourself just to drift into Mu. Take yourself in hand. Count your breaths from "one" to "ten" by way of getting yourself straight and settled. Complete each breath. Complete each count. Let each breath count. Then, when you are reasonably settled, take up Mu.

Don't suppose you are peculiar because you are forgetful, your mind drifts, and you must constantly return to your practice. We are all of us in this together.

Hsüeh-tou said, "How lamentable! So many people playing in the tide!"[38] Don't let yourself get caught in Hsüeh-tou's net!

After long days of zazen, notice that Mu is right there in your consciousness. Don't waver.

The best zazen condition is complete circumspection and honesty at the source of your thoughts. Monitor that point with Mu. Let there be only Mu — nothing else.

When you are preoccupied with sequence, you only know your consciousness up to now: "How I was, how I am, how I will be." This is the source of endless postponements. It is of the utmost importance that you come to a complete stop and settle into Mu right there.

The Jisha reminds us, "Each of us must be completely alert, / never neglectful, never indulgent."[39] It is important for us to have this reminder even though we are sitting with great determination. At the same time it is important that you see and hear and feel the message of Kuan-yin — the Kuan-yin who stands in our dokusan room. She is saving all beings, beginning with you. She is your own nature, holding a pitcher of ambrosia, not just a little receptacle, but a great big container. This ambrosia is your assurance to yourself, "I am all right to the very bottom." With the rigor of the Buddha and the self-compassion of Kuan-yin, please persevere.

The grim way — the mechanical way — won't do. There is something interesting here. Pursue that with all your heart.

The Dark Night

Sometimes you find yourself in a desert-like place where there is not a drop of water, not a blade of grass, not a bit of sustenance. Everything is dry and dreary. This is not a condition that is peculiar to the Zen path — it is described as the "sick soul" by William James in his Varieties of Religious Experience. *It is a condition of great promise. You are walking the path with all your ancestors in the Dharma, and all earnest pilgrims of religion everywhere.*

Our Tantō is sick, and is recovering upstairs while we recover downstairs. You will recall that when Vimalakīrti was ill the Buddha sent Mañjushrī and eighty-four thousand Shrāvakas, Pratyekas, and Bodhisattvas to ask after his health. After all of them had settled in his little room that was ten feet by ten feet, Mañjushrī asked, "Why are you sick?" Vimalakīrti replied, "I am sick because the whole world is sick."[40] "The sick meet the king of doctors. Why don't they recover?"[41]

Sesshin may bring on cycles of anger or fear or worry. These too are conditions, and you should regard them simply as the body that breathes Mu. At the same time, conditions can be especially noxious and difficult. Don't give way to discouragement at such times. Nothing is permanent. All things pass. Afterwards the episode will seem like a bad dream and you will be left wondering, "What was that about?" Don't give that question a second look. Just take up your practice. You will find yourself deeper and clearer as a result of the work that you did during the difficult time.

———

I am always saying that you must forget yourself and settle into Mu. This is a rather mild expression and I am afraid it evokes only a mild response. You must enter the place that David the Psalmist called "The valley of the Shadow of Death." Die to yourself as you settle into Mu. The "dark night" condition of Zen Buddhist practice is possessed of great energy. If this is your condition, use that pessimism and despair to keep yourself centered.

Nothing is static. Your understanding will unfold — it will open out.

Discouragement is no more than a condition. You ask yourself, "What in heaven's name am I doing here, counting my breaths, or repeating a meaningless syllable!" Ah, yes! Remember your vows. Don't be managed by your condition.

Robert Pirsig, in his *Zen and the Art of Motorcycle Maintenance*, speaks of the virtue of stuckness — a wonderful expression. Hsiang-yen said to his monks,

> *"It is as though you were up in a tree, hanging from a branch with your teeth. Your hands and feet can't touch any branch. Someone appears beneath the tree and asks, 'What is the meaning of Bodhidharma's coming from the West?' If you do not answer, you evade your responsibility. If you do answer, you fall to your death. What do you do?"* [42]

There in that moment you find your resolution. There is nothing to look forward to and nothing to look back upon. When you are stuck on Mu, there is nothing else — there can be nothing else. There is only that one point, so fine it isn't even there. There is only Mu inside, only Mu outside, only Mu in the whole universe. "The impeded stream sings," as Wendell Berry wrote. It is there that the gecko calls and her cousin from the neighboring home responds.

Dōgen Zenji was led into Zen practice by the question that occurred to him at the age of twelve, "Why, if all beings by nature are Buddha, was it necessary for the ancient masters to sweat blood to realize it?"[43] Well, that's the way it is. The fact that all beings by nature are Buddha makes our task easy. The fact that we have to sweat blood like the old teachers makes it hard.

Many of you are old-timers at this sesshin and the procedures are no longer a mystery. You are used to the routine. There is a certain disadvantage in being accustomed in this way. You are no longer fearful. You are no longer uncertain. Actually your confidence is a kind of defense against the ultimate fear. It is important that you open yourself again to fear, the deepest fear. Your confidence is protecting you from really coming to terms with your terror of nonbeing, which lies deep in every human heart. So practice in a spirit of vulnerability, of openness.

If you must sit on a seiza bench, then you sit on a seiza bench. If you must sit in a chair, then you sit in a chair. If you have back trouble and must lie down, then you lie down. But as the Duke says in *Measure for Measure*, "Be absolute for death, and life and death will thereby be the sweeter."

As our sesshin deepens, some of you are encountering despair and fear. Nakagawa Sōen Rōshi said to me in his inimitable English, "Don't care if you fall into hell." Step by step, Mu by Mu, walk on.

Simple and Clear

There is no magic involved in Zen practice. You do not pursue stale practice, and then suddenly find everything pure and clear. Practice Mu as purely and clearly as you can. That is the nature of your Mu, with or without realization.

Someone remarked to me that zazen can be quite complex. Actually, it is a natural function like eating. When you are hungry, you sit down and raise food to your lips. When you want to find intimacy with Mu, sit down and breathe Mu. Yüan-wu said, "Among the sixteen kinds of meditation, the baby's practice is the best." [44]

The last days of the sesshin are very precious, very powerful — with all that zazen behind you. But it is especially important now to forget about time. Settle into this breath-moment — this breath — Mu. Forget everything else, "like a fish, like a fool." [45] As you stand here, notice that there is no time. This is the unconscious place. Breathe Mu there.

Someone asked me what kind of presentation to make in the dokusan room. I said, "Keep it simple." I would say the same if I were asked about zazen. Only Mu. " 'Tis a gift to be simple."

Good health — physical, mental, spiritual — is a matter of simplicity. "Blessed are the poor in spirit." If complex things come up, let them go by. Keep your practice altogether uncomplicated. You can find the presence of Mu with just a single exhalation. Face your Mu — but stay out of its way. What is Mu?

After you have done zazen for a while, you no longer need to impose on your practice. Just keep the twigs and clods from the trail. Clear the way and your practice with its accumulated power will pursue its course.

Your practice is waiting to breathe. Absent yourself and let it ripen. Let it mature. Let there be only Mu, as clearly as you can. If you are breathing Mu mechanically, just by habit, then perhaps many thoughts are playing their games as well.

You needn't force anything. Encourage your practice. This is a time for you to use the concentration you have accumulated, and to use all sounds as reminders — the wind, the neighbors, cars going by. This is your context, this is your body. Focus with that body rigorously on Mu, on each breath you count.

I was reflecting that this sesshin is going smoothly. Too smoothly, perhaps. Tum te dum te dum. You are used to the sesshin routine. Time is passing and with the passing of time you might find yourself anticipating what comes next. You know that at a certain point we will have supper or a break, and you look forward to it. This kind of habituation and expectation is another black beast of practice. Forget yourself. Follow the signals — stay with Mu, and let everything else go. Keep your Mu new with each breath. When the Jisha calls out, "Life-and-death is a grave matter; / all things pass quickly away," do you turn her off because you have heard it before? Each time it is very important.

One, two, three, four, five, six — be careful. Don't let the practice go stale. Keep each point fresh and new. Attention! Attention!

Bankei Zenji said, "Don't put your distractions to work."[46] You meet distractions at the surface of your mind and you meet them in the deepest dream state. It is at the surface, however, that distractions can be most pernicious, though they are not in themselves bad. Speculation about realization, rehearsal of upcoming dokusan — such distractions are natural; just don't give them any energy. As Suzuki Shunryū Rōshi said, "Don't invite them for tea." Settle into Mu and let everything else go.

Nan-ch'üan said: "Among students of the Way, fools and dullards are hard to come by."[47] Fortunately, there have been a few, after all.

Zazen is very simple. Notice your present condition as you listen to my words. Are there any contending thoughts there? Sustain this easy kind of concentration in your practice.

Like a Dream

The Diamond Sutra *and many other sutras say, "Life is a dream."*[48] *One of the Diamond Sangha treasures is a plaque incised with Yamamoto Gempō Rōshi's calligraphy of the word "dream," made when he was ninety-five years old. Why should he choose "dream" as his teaching after all those years?*

In your practice, when you find yourself in a dreamlike condition with strange images coming and going, hold fast to Mu, hold fast to your breath-counting, and let the process unfold.

T. S. Eliot in "Preludes" uses the term "certain certainties" to refer to generic human preoccupations. Our zazen is difficult when we remain in that dimension. It is the dream world that informs our understanding. Sink into that dream.

True zazen does not have the hard edges of time and place. It is rather a dream of Dōgen Zenji, his ancestors, and his followers, including you and me — sitting and walking together. In that ancient dimension, so ancient that it is timeless, settle into Mu.

When you try to do zazen in the midst of contending thoughts about your family or your work or your school, then practice is very difficult. But if you sink into the dimension of dreams and focus there on Mu, on the question of who is hearing, or on counting your breaths, then you don't know where you are, really. When the umpan sounds, you don't know if it is announcing breakfast or the noon meal. This is truly forgetting yourself and uniting with your practice.

Our sesshin has become mature. Someone said to me, "I find a mythic quality in our kinhin." You can trust such an intimation. As a matter of fact, a pragmatic approach to zazen can be very difficult, but when you sense that you are walking hand-in-hand with all the ancestral teachers in the successive generations of your lineage.[49] you drop all the obstacles of time and space. You are left with a dream of Chao-chou and a monk who asks about a dog. You are left with a dream of Mu.

Hsüeh-feng said, "When I pick it up, this whole great earth is like a grain of rice in size."[50] This is only possible in a dream.

If you are truly focused on your practice, then there is no inside and no outside, and Buddha nature pervades the whole universe. The faraway dog is barking Mu in your heart.

The Last Night

After dokusan is over for the evening, the Rōshi enters the dōjō, there is a little ceremony of bells, drum, and han, the Rōshi offers a few words, everyone makes three bows to the floor, and then bells signal the end of the day. Percussion ends our day. Percussion enlightens all beings.

When I stepped into the dōjō this evening, I was struck by how deeply all of you are confirmed in your practice. Truly you are touching the mind. Please persevere.

Listen to the peace of this dōjō as you stand here. This peace is not the opposite of violence, but the pure peace of breathing in and out. There is only the hum of the freeway in the infinite void — no thoughts at all. Please retire in that peace.

We come now to the last night of our sesshin, a time when the rules are relaxed, and you are welcome to sit up. Make your bed, and then come back down to the dōjō and take your seat. It is all voluntary, with no bells or clappers. Sit as long as you wish, do kinhin when you wish. This is yaza, night sitting, a very pleasant practice, sitting quietly in the atmosphere of Mu and allowing the fruit of the sesshin to ripen. When you are tired, just go to bed. If you have any question about whether or not you should sit up, please go to bed immediately. Tomorrow is another day.[51]

As you stand here quietly breathing, notice the steady beam of the samādhi you have cultivated over these several days of zazen. Stay on that beam with your Mu.

It is not that you have a Buddha mind and a delusive mind. The Buddha mind is really not the Buddha mind. Whatever it is, keep it constant.

You have been sitting hard all day today, and tonight and tomorrow extend before you. Indeed time extends endlessly, but you can find the timeless in a single moment. Look straight ahead as you lower your eyelids. There is no time there because there are no thoughts.

Afterword

When I come into the dōjō for the ceremony at the end of sesshin, I sometimes recall the story I heard at Ryūtakuji about monks long ago at the end of a sesshin. They were filled with enthusiasm and elected to sit on for another seven days. I know the feeling, and I think most students have experienced it. All that effort to concentrate and get settled on Mu is at last beginning to pay off — and now ironically the sesshin is coming to an end. "Shall we sit another seven days?" After the most minute hesitation everyone will say, "Well, no, not this time. Let's move on." The cycle of intensive work is phasing out, and now we must find ways to apply our good work.

Intimacy is the quality of our practice and of our realization. Please remember this as you return to your home and job.

You have survived on zazen during these many days, and you are probably more tired than you feel. Allow yourself to come down naturally. Make rest your practice now, and avoid talk that is excessively analytical. Keep yourself simple, as the Buddha mind is simple.

As you return to your lives in the world, please treat the difficulties you meet the way you treat them in sesshin. Each difficulty has its own quality and must be handled appropriately, but generally speaking, difficulties are there to be suffered, that is to say, allowed. Please don't treat them as adversaries. Difficulties are the context of your life.

Find intervals during your workaday life when you can practice one-breath Mu. Listen to the peace without and within. This is the place where you practice zazen and breathe Mu. This is the place where you greet the post office clerk and embrace your children.

One of my friends works in an office where the workers tend to neglect each other's feelings. He has made it his conscious practice to encourage harmony among them. He is a Bodhisattva who does not limit his wisdom and compassion to bowing in the dōjō. He proves the Buddha's teaching each mindful moment.

The place of integrity is the source of your thoughts.

NOTES

1. Hee Jin Kim, *Dōgen Kigen: Mystical Realist* (Tucson: University of Arizona Press, 1987), pp. 61–62.

2. Robert Aitken, *The Gateless Barrier: The Wu-men kuan (Mumonkan)*, translated and with a commentary (San Francisco: North Point Press, 1990), pp. 39–41.

3. The first of the Four Noble Truths. See Walpola Rahula, *What the Buddha Taught* (New York: Grove Press, 1959), pp. 16–50.

4. Koken Murano, *The Buddha and His Disciples* (Tokyo: Sanyusha, 1932), p. viii.

5. In this instance, in Adelaide, South Australia.

6. Cf. William F. Powell, *The Record of Tung-shan* (Honolulu: University of Hawaii Press, 1986), p. 62.

7. Aitken, *The Gateless Barrier*, p. 9.

8. Syllabus, The Zen Buddhist Sutra Book: "First Sutra Service Dedication" (these lines were translated by Nakagawa Sōen Rōshi from the traditional dedication).

9.   Syllabus, The Zen Buddhist Sutra Book: "Hakuin Zenji: 'Song of Zazen.'"

10.   See Daisetz T. Suzuki, *Manual of Zen Buddhism* (New York: Grove Press, 1960), p. 155.

11.   John Blofeld, trans., *The Zen Teachings of Instant Awakening by Hui Hai* (Leicester: Buddhist Publishing Group, 1987), p. 24.

12.   Aitken, *The Gateless Barrier*, p. 126.

13.   Kim, *Dōgen Kigen*, p. 34.

14.   Syllabus, The Zen Buddhist Sutra Book: "Evening Message."

15.   Aitken, *The Gateless Barrier*, p. 179.

16.   Syllabus, The Zen Buddhist Sutra Book: "Emmei Jikku Kannon Gyō."

17.   Powell, *The Record of Tung-shan*, p. 49.

18.   Syllabus, *Wu-men kuan*, Case I: "Wu-men's Comment."

19.   Ibid.

20.   See note 8.

21.   Simone Weil, "Reflections on the Right Use of School Studies with a View to the Love of God," in George A. Panichas, *The Simone Weil Reader* (New York: David McKay Company, 1977), pp. 47–48.

22.   Cf. Yoel Hoffman, *Radical Zen: The Sayings of Jōshū* (Brookline, Mass.: Autumn Press, 1979), p. 107.

23.   Cf. Haku'un Yasutani, "Introductory Lectures on Zen Training," in Philip Kapleau, *The Three Pillars of Zen: Teaching, Practice, and Enlightenment* (Boston: Beacon Press, 1965), p. 28.

24.   Ch'ang-sha Ch'ing-ts'en, quoted by Wu-men Hui-k'ai in the *Wu-men kuan*. See Aitken, *The Gateless Barrier*, pp. 81, 87, 297.

25.   Aitken, *The Gateless Barrier*, pp. 7–9.

26.   Ibid., p. 7.

27.   See Robert Aitken, *Taking the Path of Zen* (San Francisco: North Point Press, 1982), pp. 110–11.

28. Syllabus, The Zen Buddhist Sutra Book: "Hakuin Zenji: 'Song of Zazen.'"

29. Cf. Powell, *The Record of Tung-shan*, p. 62.

30. Syllabus, The Zen Buddhist Sutra Book: "Evening Service Dedication."

31. See Syllabus, The Zen Buddhist Sutra Book: "Hakuin Zenji: 'Song of Zazen.'"

32. Murano, *The Buddha and His Disciples*, p. viii.

33. See Syllabus, The Zen Buddhist Sutra Book: "Evening Service Dedication."

34. I have enlarged upon Hakuin's words. See Philip Yampolsky, *The Zen Master Hakuin: Selected Writings* (New York: Columbia, 1971), p. 84.

35. Cf. Powell, *The Record of Tung-shan*, p. 61.

36. See Richard A. Gard, *Buddhism* (New York: George Braziller, 1962), pp. 52–53.

37. Syllabus, The Zen Buddhist Sutra Book: "Great Vows for All."

38. Thomas Cleary and J. C. Cleary, *The Blue Cliff Record* (Boston: Shambhala, 1992), pp. 516–18.

39. Syllabus, The Zen Buddhist Sūtra Book: "The Dedications and the Evening Message."

40. Charles Luk, *The Vimalakīrti Nirdesa Sūtra* (Boston: Shambhala, 1990), p. 50.

41. "Cheng-tao ke." Cf. Nyogen Senzaki and Ruth Strout McCandless, *Buddhism and Zen* (San Francisco: North Point Press, 1987), p. 54.

42. Aitken, *The Gateless Barrier*, p. 38.

43. See "Words from the Rōshi," note 2.

44. Cleary and Cleary, *The Blue Cliff Record*, p. 521.

45. Syllabus, Dōjō Percussion Instruments: "The Han."

46.   Norman Waddell, trans., *The Unborn: The Life and Teachings of Zen Master Bankei* (San Francisco: North Point Press, 1984), p. 119.

47.   Cleary and Cleary, *The Blue Cliff Record*, p. 169.

48.   A. F. Price, *The Diamond Sutra*, p. 74, in *The Diamond Sutra and The Sutra of Hui Neng* (Berkeley: Shambhala, 1969).

49.   Aitken, *The Gateless Barrier*, p. 7.

50.   Cleary and Cleary, *The Blue Cliff Record*, p. 31.

51.   Sesshin ends at noon on the last day.

Words from the Rōshi

INTRODUCTION

"Words from the Rōshi" are little essays I composed for newsletters of the Diamond Sangha, first at the Maui Zendō, beginning about 1977, and then from 1984 onward at the Koko An Zendō in Honolulu. They were intended as pieces for particular times and places, and in a serial collection they show changes in Western Zen Buddhism and in my own views. Some reflect steps in our centers toward establishing a moral code that is based upon clearly enunciated, but relatively undeveloped principles found in the tradition. Others are concerned more generally with our task of establishing our religion in the West and in fulfilling our vow to save the many beings.

My original inspiration in Zen Buddhism was R. H. Blyth's *Zen in English Literature and Oriental Classics,** and I am still inclined

---

* R. H. Blyth, *Zen in English Literature and Oriental Classics* (New York: Dutton, 1960).

to explore those elements of Western culture that seem to touch perennial depths where Zen Buddhism too can be discerned. Thus a number of the essays touch on European or American ideas that I find related to my Zen path.

Finally, still other essays reflect my concern that we keep in touch with the ancient. We turn the wheel of the Dharma in our time and place in the most relevant manner possible, but the wheel itself is the one turned by the Buddha.

We have negative models from the past that offer guidance for this task. On the one hand, Ōbaku Zen Buddhism, which was really a reintroduction of Lin-chi Buddhism into Japan after it had become mixed with Pure Land practices, has remained a Chinese island in Japanese culture. Sutras are recited in the Chinese manner with the Chinese tones, monks dress in Chinese robes, and even affect Chinese caps and Chinese-style beards. The sect has remained small and generally unappealing. On the other hand, when Lin-chi Zen first was introduced into Japan, Chinese masters in Kamakura found that their samurai followers disliked foreign influences. Accordingly they made a study of Japanese culture and made up kōans from episodes in Japanese history and folklore so that the samurai would be more comfortable with the practice. It was too hurried an adjustment and did not work out well. Succeeding Japanese masters returned for the most part to Chinese archetypal cases.

So we must find the Middle Way, which is neither a matter of stiffly retaining nor of carelessly abandoning. Nor is it merely some kind of adjustment between extremes. The very heart of the Great Matter is the Middle Way. Making that heart our own and keeping in touch with our friends we can express our gratitude with the utmost cogency.

The Middle Way

1990

Early in this century, physicists began using the word "complementarity" to show how light can be discussed in terms of both waves and particles, even though these two descriptions seem to contradict each other. "Complementarity" can also be used when speaking about many other apparent contradictions, being and nonbeing for example. The nature of the self is another complementarity — ego and non-ego.

Ego and non-ego form a complementarity that can be explained mathematically, so to speak, but in our lives the subject of research is not "out there" and is, in fact, the observer herself or himself. The burden of proof is not upon research instruments, but upon the conduct of the self. If the observer behaves egotistically, then the teaching of ego as non-ego is mocked.

This teaching is not, however, a denial of ego, any more than emptiness is a denial of form. "Form is exactly emptiness; / emptiness is exactly form," as the "Heart Sutra" says.[1] Ego is exactly non-ego; non-ego exactly ego. You and I are each of us unique, with potentials that are yours and mine to fulfill. At the same time, there is no abiding self; nothing to be called "soul" that is fixed during life and goes prowling around after death to search for new parents. The qualities that come together by mysterious affinities to form you or me or the guava bush form selves that are insubstantial, yet here we are!

The challenge of our practice on our cushions is to realize this most intimate complementarity by experience. The challenge of our practice in daily life is to present this same complementarity while, for example, we gradually give our children independence. No thing abides; substance is only a dream. We dance as Shiva the mystery and joy of the Buddha Sangha — the trackless wilderness and the planets on their course.

———

"If all beings by nature are Buddha, why did our ancestors have to work so hard for realization?" This was the problem Dōgen Zenji faced as a young monk. It is said that when he questioned Eisai Zenji about it, Eisai replied, "Our ancestors did not know that all beings by nature are Buddha. Only the otter and white bull know such a thing." [2]

If someone came to me with such a question, I might answer, "Because they were honest like you."

Dōgen's question can also be asked in the world. If everything is all right from the beginning, why should I exert myself socially? The most profound peace has been here from the beginning. Why should Gandhi have bothered? He was honest too.

Is Zen a religion? Many teachers say "No." In an issue of *Blind Donkey*, Father Willigis Jäger makes a convincing case for "No." [3]

I agree. "When you meet the Buddha, you kill the Buddha." [4]

Is Zen just a humanist path? I don't think it can be. I think "When you meet the Buddha, you kill the Buddha" means that old fellow has already disappeared and is safely ensconced as the one who stands at the window.

1991

Two crossed swords, neither permitting retreat,
dexterously wielded, like a lotus amidst fire —
the natural determination to ascend the heavens. [5]

This is Mode Four of Tung-shan's *Five Modes of the Particular and the Universal*. It presents the particular thing in tension with the particular thing, the fundamental tension that is life itself.

"Lotus amidst fire" — this familiar Buddhist phrase is commonly understood to mean that realization can flower in difficult circumstances. This is not a mistaken interpretation, but it is not precise enough.

The lotus is purity and fire is the heat of desires. You yearn to be pure, but yearning without heat is merely latent aspiration. On the other hand, fire without vows can be destructive, for fire consumes all, and can get out of hand very quickly.

Furthermore, without the imperative to be pure, you would be awash in indulgence. Without the power of desire, you would be isolated in a cave of asceticism. The tension between the fire and the lotus is the Middle Way. This Middle Way is not a compromise, but "the natural determination to ascend the heavens," the noblest possible aspiration, which we share with the trees.

The lotus is also realization — wisdom. Here again, two conflicting imperatives cross swords creatively. On the one hand there is conventional wisdom that encourages making a career of the self, and on the other there is the Buddha Way. Forgetting the self you cultivate the self. Once again this is the tension of the ultimate path.

In the Buddha Sangha, there are many such creative tensions that are themselves maturity. For example, we feel a conflict between our need to maintain family and job with our need to devote all possible time and energy to religious practice. That's it! That very conflict itself! The highest and best! Similar supreme encounters are found between egalitarian imperatives and the authority necessary to convey the Buddha Dharma; between personal needs and the needs of the community; and between sectarian interchange and the exploration of a single path.

These tensions are the threads of our life fabric. Existence is not the warp alone — you need threads going both ways. Just as there is no asceticism without desire, so there is also no life-practice without children. Tradition is not valid unless it is relevant, and individual attainment is vain without group fulfillment.

The partisan cannot find the Middle Way and remains forever and ever stuck in the immaturity of a single side. At the same time, you can't be all things to all women and men. Our task is to be as clear as we can about the issues and as rigorous as we can about our limitations and potentials — then to agree to disagree while we work together to be as wise and as inclusive as our collective nature will allow.

1991

Some people consider Zen Buddhism to be anti-intellectual. But the Buddha, Te-shan, Hsiang-yen, and many others among our ancestors were accomplished philosophers before they took up the practice of zazen. When they became teachers, their powerful intellects gave marvelous articulation to their enlightenment. The Middle Way is the path of integrating knowledge and experience, wisdom and compassion.

1992

Time and no time, substance and the void, existence and nonexistence — these are the traditional dyads of the human program. With zazen we find the Middle Way and the hoary concepts of dimension drop away.

Using the Self

1979

To use the self is to forget it. Anxiety turns into purposeful action. Brooding disappears, daydreaming disappears. All beings enrich the universe with uniquely varied creativity. Our experiences in practice, education, and realization function in synergy to give that enrichment its fullest possible blessing. It is the self forgotten that achieves this.

1980

Meister Eckhart says, "The truth is that the more ourselves we are, the less self is in us." [6] This is the meaning of "true self." It is honesty at the very source of thoughts. It cannot be reached by self-admonition, but only by attention to the task at hand.

1981

In the *Ts'ai-ken t'an*, a seventeenth-century Chinese book of brief essays and fables, we find the passage,

> *The wind blows through a bamboo grove, and the trunks clatter together. When it has passed, the grove is silent once more. Geese crossing the sky are reflected in a cold, deep pool. When they are gone, no trace remains. For the sage, when something comes, it appears in the mind. When it goes, the mind returns to the void.* [7]

We can test our practice with these metaphors. "What is it that does not die down in my mind?" Ask yourself that. It will probably turn out to be something which centers on yourself.

1982

When I was a teacher of creative writing, I had a hard time persuading my students to treat their first drafts as something preliminary. They thought of them as something sacred that could not be touched. With this emotional investment, they were unable to finish their work.

We all have this problem. When we do something, we feel

obliged to defend our action. When we say something, we will then argue from those words as though they formed an irrefutable premise.

Yet our teacher Shākyamuni is still doing zazen and really is only halfway to complete enlightenment. Keep yourself open to correction, open to change. This is the Buddha Tao.

1982

Yamada Rōshi has said, "The purpose of Zen is to forget the self in the act of uniting with something." Zazen is our model — forgetting everything except Mu. This model inspires Buddha's action in the world. You devote your energy to your task, your personal preoccupations are forgotten and the appropriate option becomes clear.

There is nothing in the way when you forget yourself.

1983

All things reflect, interpenetrate, and indeed contain all other things. This is the organic nature of the universe, and is called mutual interdependence in classical Buddhism.[8] Affinity and co-incidence are its surface manifestations. The philosophy of Alfred North Whitehead, the theories of modern physics, the *Hua-yen Sutra*, and the experience of the Zen student — all are expressive of this most fundamental truth: the other is no other than myself. This is the foundation of the precepts and the inspiration for genuine human behavior.

To acknowledge one's own dark side with a smile and to acknowledge the shining side of the other person with a smile — this is practice. Keeping the shining side of one's self always in view and holding fast to the dark side of the other — this is not practice. It enforces self-preoccupation and is destructive of the Buddha Sangha. Kuan-yin weeps. Time passes.

1985

The *Ts'ai-ken t'an* says:

> *"If treacherous talk is constantly in your ears, and un-wanted thoughts are constantly in your mind, you can turn these about and use them as whetstones to enhance your practice. If every word that came to your ears were agreeable, and all things in your mind were pleasant, then your whole life would be poisoned and wasted."*[9]

"The one who praises me is a thief; the one who criticizes me is my true friend." There are several possible ways this Chinese proverb might be considered to be untrue. For example, the criticism might tend to undermine my self-confidence at an important time, or the person who criticizes might just be dumping self-centered feelings.

Nonetheless, it is a proverb that can also be considered always to be true. Criticism to one's face comes rarely. It is a chance to come to a full stop and reflect as objectively as possible. Am I on the right path?

1987

The Great Way is obvious to all my friends. They point it out quite readily on request, sometimes without request. Their words are painful because they threaten my character. I have to choose between the Great Way and me. An easy choice on paper — a hard one in fact.

Buddhist practice subverts the ordinary tendencies of the self and society. It undermines greed with generosity; hatred with compassion; self-preoccupation with the search for truth.

Probably one of the commonest questions asked in the dokusan room is about effort. Nakagawa Sōen Rōshi used to say that such questions are difficult and he would let it go at that. Yamada Kōun Rōshi would say that you must use effort but it should not be muscular effort.

I agree with Yamada Rōshi and I sympathize with Nakagawa Rōshi but I have long felt that the question itself needs to be examined. It is like Chao-chou asking Nan-ch'üan how he could come to know the Tao unless he directed himself toward it. Nan-ch'üan explained that the Tao is not subject to knowing or not knowing.[10]

It would also be possible to respond to the young Chao-chou by asking, "What is your purpose?" If Chao-chou's answer showed clear aspiration, then Nan-ch'üan would be left with nothing to say. The aspiration to understand essential nature, to stand beneath it, so to speak, and make it one's own — that in itself is effort. It will direct all one's practice, on cushions and everywhere else.

Aspiration for the Tao is Bodhichitta, the Thought of Enlightenment, or Enlightenment in Mind. This is the foundation of Buddhist practice, as our ancestors have said from the beginning. It is not a matter of setting goals. Nan-ch'üan cautioned Chao-chou not to maintain some *thing* called Tao as his purpose.

Rather, the aspiring mind is itself the Tao, the mind of practice is itself enlightenment, as Dōgen Zenji keeps telling us. This mind is with us all the while and we engage its power when we recall how briefly we are here. It just needs a nudge here and there, as Nan-ch'üan's words nudged Chao-chou, as the child who is learning the trumpet next door nudges us.

Recently I've been reading about Shamanism in my spare time, both in primary sources like *Black Elk Speaks,* and in secondary ones, such as *Teachings from the American Earth.* This latter work contains an essay by Benjamin Lee Whorf on Hopi metaphysics, linguistics, and religious practice that is instructive for Zen students.

Like other Native Americans, the Hopi cultivates the sacred in the everyday world. This cultivation is called "hope" or "hoping" and the term is used not only for human aspiration but for "the growing of plants, the forming of clouds and their condensation in rain, the careful planning out of the communal activities of agriculture and architecture and in all human hoping, wishing, striving and taking thought, and most especially concentrated in prayer, the constant hopeful praying of the Hopi community . . . which conducts the pressure of the collective Hopi thought and will out of the subjective into the objective." [11]

The objective is the sacred reality of the universe, true by nature. The basic meaning of the word which Whorf translates as "hope" is subjective activity or force, and the fulfillment of "hope" is "coming true." Thus we see how Bodhichitta, the longing for enlightenment, is perennially human, and perennially biological.

Ordinary Mind Is the Tao

1987

When Nan-ch'üan told Chao-chou that ordinary mind is the Tao, he also said that such a mind is vast and boundless — like outer space. [12] For most people, however, the vast and boundless mind would not seem to be at all ordinary.

The point is that ordinary, everyday mind is the mind that has nothing extraneous. There is no preoccupation lurking in the shadows to link up with a thought or perception.

When there are no preoccupations, then, as the Buddha said, we can realize the sacred nature of people, animals, and plants. But almost everyone is preoccupied with protecting and expanding the self, and thus excluding or even exploiting others. Each self is encircled and vastness is confined to the calculations of astronomers.

1988

In the Diamond Sangha we often repeat Yamada Kōun Rōshi's dictum: "The purpose of Zen is the perfection of character." This does not mean becoming another character, for that is not possible. It means nurturing your own qualities and making this fulfillment your life.

One of my old classmates, who became a colleague in the years when I was on the staff of the University of Hawaii, used to complain about his dreams. "Other people have inspired, witty dreams," he would say. "I just go to the store and see the merchandise laid out neatly in little compartments. My dreams are so boring — I must be a boring fellow."

Well, he was never boring, though as one might expect, he was always highly organized. He has trained school counselors for more than thirty years, and is highly regarded in his field.

The inspiration is in the merchandise, and my old friend has many jewels in his offerings. I think he has probably acknowledged them by now, in his modest way. This kind of acknowledgment can take a long time, and in the process self-doubts can be troublesome.

If you can accept yourself as you are, then you can develop your merchandise, your offering, for others to enjoy. It will be displayed in your own setting.

Individuality and ego are commonly denied by Bodhisattvas who are just entering the Path. I sometimes receive letters in which it is obvious that the writer has gone to great lengths to avoid the pronouns "I" and "me," and indeed all the pronouns. The passive voice rules — for example, "For the first time the Rōshi is hearing from this direction" — rather than "I have not written to you before." I want to say with T'ou-tzu, "Come out in the daylight!" [13] Be yourself, just as you are! The individuality, uniqueness, and variety of persons, animals, plants, and things — this is the wealth of the universe. I offer my riches, you offer yours.

As Jesus said, the candle belongs on a candlestick so that the household may be given light. It does not belong under a bushel. You and I offer ourselves. We make ourselves available. Like the hibiscus or the thrush, we announce, "Take me! I have something to give! Help me to make this giving possible!"

More about giving: During our childhood years it is not at all clear that giving is the function of life. One of my earliest memories is a Christmas with my grandparents. I heard my grandmother say, "It is more blessed to give than to receive." I didn't think that was right at all. It was obvious to me, sitting there happily opening my presents, that it was much more blessed to receive than to give. This is the natural, childish mind.

Now as an adult, I see my grandmother's point, and accordingly I would like to offer a modest correction to the Buddhist concept of interdependence. It seems to me that "interdependence" implies that I receive from you, and you receive from me. If it is more blessed to give than to receive, then "intersupport" would surely be a better term. I give to you, and you give to me. This is eternal, everyday harmony — eternal, everyday practice.

Still, giving and receiving are the same act from different directions. If it is hard for a child to understand giving — and if giving still takes practice for the adult — it is hard also to receive graciously. The term "Thank you" in Japanese means literally, "I have difficulty."

1989

I vow to open the Buddha's eyes to the Morning Star and to acknowledge each being including stones and leaves as fully realized. This is experiential, metaphysical, and practical.

The experiential opening is the acceptance of myself and others as sacred. "I and all beings have in this moment attained the Way." [14]

The metaphysical opening is the knowledge which becomes evident with experience. The Buddha, musing under the Bodhi tree after his realization, is our archetype. It became clear to him that the self is without substance — the human self, the animal and plant selves. It also became clear that everything serves everything else and that one thing leads to another.

The practical opening is a path of fulfilled enlightenment, as Dōgen Zenji said. [15] This is the Eightfold Path of liberation and the Way of the Bodhisattva to save the many beings. It is the work of the unknown Buddha, with a pot, a telephone, a pencil, a spade.

1991

The Great Way is the noble path of the realized human being, but everybody knows about it. Mencius said, "The Way is like a great highroad; there is no difficulty whatsoever in recognizing it. What is wrong with us is that we do not really search for it. Just go home, and plenty of people will point it out to you." [16]

Plenty of people know about perennial truth. I speak so often of perennial truth that I wear out the words. But perennial truth itself cannot wear out. It is the mind of stones and clouds — the mind in harmony with the stones and clouds, animals and plants. It is the mind in harmony with human bodies and brains. We as human beings, perhaps uniquely of all species, have the talent to realize this mind — to see into its mirror and find the face that is no other than our own.

There is a scale of consciousness that runs from blind integration to conscious separation, with stones at one extreme, cats and kangaroos somewhere in the middle, and human beings at odds with themselves at the other extreme. Off the scale is the re-integrated human being, who has attended to the wisdom of sages.

Who are the sages? You needn't look far. As our sutra dedication says, "Our friends and family members guide us as we walk the ancient path." When they pause at their tillers or woks or business lunches and point out the way to the capital, pay attention! Their common sense is the nature of our consciousness, our con-science, the sense we have together. It is the wisdom of stones and clouds transmuted to human flesh. It is the mind, of every single day of all time, and in the dimension of no time.

On the other hand, it is the unusual mind that worries about how I am, how I was, how I will be. The unusual mind is the tape of the me-me monologue, ephemera of ephemera, not in any sense except the antinomian the every-day mind, for one day all too soon it will disappear completely — never, ever to be heard from again.

All those hoary sayings like "It's a dog-eat-dog world" and "I've got mine, Jack" are simply expressions on the me-me tape that appeal to other self-demonstrators. Such platitudes, "flat as a plate," do not express commonality except as a conspiracy of narcissism. They serve simply to hold me to what Keats called the sole self, the center that must prove itself superior to all other centers, over and over, to the very last breath of oxygen through a tube.

What is my practice? What is your practice? You and I can practice the sole self, or we can practice the multi-centered self. Our lives are our practice.

———

Our teachers are not limited to Chao-chou, Yün-men, et al. Recently I have had occasion to look again at the work of Frederick Franck, disciple of Albert Schweitzer, Pope John, Daisetz T. Suzuki and his own genius. His writing and his art instruct our practice, on our cushions and in our daily life.

Franck writes: "It has often been said that the word 'religion' derives from the Latin 'religare,' to bind together. Reflecting on what this 'binding together' might mean, I concluded that . . . the term 'religion' refers to a picking up of the pieces — to a gluing together of what was broken and fragmented — to re-storing the shards of my fragmented existence in order to attain, what? To attain my wholeness as a person. But more than that: to bring about my integration into the greater wholeness of the human community, and from there into that of the biosphere of our Earth." [17]

What is the process by which one picks up the pieces and restores wholeness? In a catalog of Franck's recent paintings and drawings, the critic Frans Boenders wrote that Franck's drawing is an act which brings the latent into the open: "He helps it being born, as if he were a midwife . . . tenderly respecting its intactness, its dignity, one might even say its sacredness." [18] I am reminded of John Donne in "The Crosse":

> *Carvers do not faces make,*
> *But that away, which hid them there, do take.*

Boenders continues: "One wonders what the artist gains from these in-scapes, and can only conclude that it must be the satisfaction of a work well done, a process brought to its conclusion. Ultimately, however, it may be his way to liberation, to a kind of salvation."

In other words, Frederick Franck's painting and drawing bring forth all he meets, and thus his art brings forth himself. He inspires people, animals, and plants, landscapes, seas and clouds to become truly themselves. He fulfills the first Bodhisattva Vow, to save the many beings as his own self-realization. There are, of course, many other ways to save the many beings and oneself but all can be guided by this marvelous octogenarian, whose message is many-layered, yet ultimately simple: "No one ever becomes adult," he wrote, but "becomes either delightfully childlike or pitifully juvenile." [19]

Cycles and Stages

1978

Our training period begins today, and our beginning is the model for our work throughout the next three months.

Each breath is a beginning, each moment a start.

There is currently much interest in the subject of dying, a healthy interest, for it has been a taboo subject in recent times. Raymond A. Moody has written a fascinating account of his interviews with people who experienced something near death and then returned to life. On musing over this book (*Life After Life*, Bantam Books, 1977), I am moved once again by the mystery of being a human being. How recklessly people neglect this mystery!

1979

"Perfection" is a noun describing an ultimate state, a light on our path shining from highest ideals. When used in the phrase, "the perfection of," it becomes an action, a becoming. Becoming is also an ultimate state — the best we can unfold at this time.

The traditional way of perfection in the Zen school is through zazen, dokusan, teishō, and Sangha interaction. I do not, however, think that we should be limited to traditional Zen ways to engage in this becoming. For example, in dealing with emotions, Theravada and Vajrayana teach us how to examine feelings directly, to see that they are empty. Psychology handles feelings in a similar way.

Sometimes, by personal quirks of character, we get stale and discouraged, following a single sectarian path. There is no need to be limited. I think that as Zen students we can learn from other traditions without violating our own. I wish to encourage you to examine tools used by people outside Zen Buddhism, with a view to their possible incorporation into your own practice. I think you should be open to all possible ways to fulfill your Great Vows.

How to handle ourselves right after sesshin is a question all of us are in process of resolving. At some Zen centers, there is a big party, and people get stoned one way or another. I personally don't feel comfortable with this way of coming down. It is an empirical matter, however. What is best for your practice in the long run?

In any case, I am sure that the first few days after sesshin are especially important. With the kind of socializing you find rewarding, you will also need plenty of rest, plenty of peace and quiet, with lots of zazen. Then the wonderful virtue of sesshin will have a chance to take root.

Commonly we hear that zazen is a lifetime practice. We may suppose that this means we should do zazen every day for the rest of our lives. But zazen is also a matter of devotion to each task. And a lifetime is all of it contained in the single act of plumping up a zafu.

The realized mind is the mind of nurturing.

I have been asked, "How should I maintain my practice now that the training period is over?" My response to this question is no different from my answer to questions about practice during training periods.

I do have one suggestion, however. You can read. In addition to daily zazen and to mindful attention to workaday activities, books are very useful upāya. There are many good Zen Buddhist titles now. Follow your nose as you prowl in your bookstore. Pull down books and activate your sense of smell. You'll find the one or two that suit you at this time. Reading short selections aloud every day is effective Dharma work.

1981

Practice is twofold. The first part is training; the second is the act itself. And these are not two things: when you train, the act itself is happening; when you are the act itself, your training is deepened.

Practice is to work "as if." The lawyer practices as if she or he were an attorney. The doctor practices as if she or he were a physician. Being and learning are one and the same.

It is just as though you were trying to play the piano with Mozart's hands. At first such action "as if" is awkward, but with practice your music becomes your own best creation. In the same way, your zazen becomes your own best inspiration, and your interaction with others expresses the love which has been in your heart from the very beginning.

Recently I read a statement by a Japanese Buddhist attacking Zen as a "porno" religion. He meant that with all the emphasis on kenshō, the initial realization, we have reduced our religion to a kind of sensation.

There are two observations I would like to make about this. The first is that indeed there is too much talk about kenshō. Zen Buddhism is a lifetime practice involving deeper and clearer insights to the very point of holding hands with your loved ones and saying good-bye for the last time.

The second point is that things always look different from the other side of the counter. The Japanese critic said what he did because he did not know what it is to be a Zen student, just as we might not know what it is to be a clerk at the checkout counter when we pass our groceries before her. Putting others in a certain box and labeling them not only violates the Sixth Precept, it gets in the way of realizing our innate kinship.

1982

In the *Paradiso,* Dante and Beatrice visit various levels of heaven and interview inhabitants there. The first level is the Moon, where they meet souls of priests and nuns who sinned grievously and were forgiven. It is very cool there, and the souls don't smile much. It is nonetheless heaven, just as higher reaches where souls are ecstatic are also heaven. One of the souls explains that all souls are receptacles and in heaven all are filled. My first teacher R. H. Blyth commented, "Some are barrels and some are thimbles."

As Zen students, we can understand this allegory to mean that one experience is slight and another is deep, but each is insight into essential nature. One may bring a smile, another a laugh, but each in its own way is joyous.

The allegory falls apart at this point, for the Zen student does not stop with one experience, but can go on to deeper and deeper understanding.

1982

Recently an old-timer came to me and complained that he no longer felt enthusiasm for his practice. I questioned him and learned that he was limiting his zazen to his visits to the

Zendō. I can understand how his enthusiasm might erode over a period of time when his zazen is limited to two sessions a week.

It is not merely enthusiasm that erodes when practice declines. Your body and mind go out of tune. You are no longer a vessel of insight. The cardinal can sing; the wind can move the ironwood trees delicately; a child can ask a wise question — and where is your center? How can you respond?

It is time to put yourself back in tune, to be ready for experiences that make life fulfilling. Take up the advice for beginners. Put your zazen pad somewhere between your bathroom and your kitchen. Sit down there in the morning after you use the bathroom and before you cook breakfast. You are sitting with everyone in the world. If you can sit only briefly, you will have at least settled your day.

No advice is easier to give than this, or harder to follow — for me too. The day stretches forth before me invitingly. Surely I can cut my zazen without harm, and get at the important stuff. One tiny decision leads to more tiny decisions, and the path is neglected.

1986

Many people work hard to retire, and then find retirement a bore, or worse. It is important to be clear about ends and means. The means you choose for some future end are here and now. They are your mode of life. You are creating your future in the way you are living your life at this moment. The ends you seek, so-called future ends, beyond present time, are guesses at best.

It is good to plan, but the planning itself is a mode of life. The question is not so much "What future do I want?" but "What mode do I want?"

———

Dōgen Zenji says:

> *You should ponder the fact that kind speech is not just
> praising the merit of others; it has the power to turn the
> destiny of the nation.*[20]

1988

From my correspondence:

"Before and during sesshin, I was laboring under a misconcep-
tion of how my practice should work: I was trying to pour effort
into my zazen, in the hope that an experience labeled 'realization'
would somehow arrive. Basically, I was hanging on to what I
thought of as a static experience belonging to a fixed moment,
believing that anything after that would somehow be 'post-
realization.'

"Then came the red-hot iron ball. Sitting with it, being aware
that I couldn't (and still can't) swallow it or spit it out, it dawned
on me that my approach to practice had been inadequate, and that
I shouldn't be passively waiting for a static realization to occur,
but rather should and can be actively, dynamically realizing Mu
in each moment, and that this is also something entirely natural
and spontaneous.

"As a result, it has become clear to me how to 'let Mu breathe
Mu': it is not a process of waiting for Mu to somehow breathe
itself, but rather of actively allowing each moment or breath to be
nothing more nor less than Mu, self-renewing, perpetual and
complete.

"Coming to this insight has deepened my practice considerably,
and it's also far clearer to me how to find my practice in everything
I do. I'm learning that Wu-men's iron ball is an overwhelming,
ongoing experience, but not a painful one as the image might
suggest. Rather it's the experience which carries everything else
with it and gives it sense."

In my response I acknowledged this milestone with warm encouragement, and then said: "Your sesshin was important preparatory work. You are in a different phase now, and this would not be possible without the effort you gave during your sesshin and before. Your earlier practice evolved to your present practice, and your present practice too will evolve. Zazen teaches zazen."

1989

Some students of religion postpone their lives and then wake up one day and say, "Wait a minute, here I am forty years old and I don't have a spouse or a career. What am I going to do when I grow up?" They have let things back up as they wait to be enlightened, or to be settled in mind. This shows a misunderstanding of the nature of practice.

Right Practice, the ninth step of the Eightfold Path, does not involve waiting for the psyche to ripen. The clock is ticking. Right Practice is taking yourself in hand. For the lay student, it can include college, a career, and a family. It is to get on with living. The confidence and maturity that comes with a productive life will enhance zazen and deepen satori.

1991

There are ten Pāramitās,[21] and every once in a while an eleventh occurs to me. This month I would like to suggest Completion as one of our Perfections.

One model of Completion is the way Japanese people say good-bye. Suppose you are leaving a home. You say good-bye in the living room, and then you say good-bye at the door. You walk down to the corner and turn around, and there in the distance are your hosts at their gate. You wave good-bye once again at that point. If you fail to turn around at the corner, your hosts will feel that their good-bye process was cut off before its completion and they will be disappointed.

I remember once going to Haneda airport with Nakagawa Sōen Rōshi to say good-bye to Charles Gooding, a fellow student who was returning to the United States. It was pouring rain, but the Rōshi insisted upon standing on the unprotected balcony of the airport after Charley had boarded, to wave good-bye to the airplane until it took off. Ridiculous, perhaps, but quite instructive.

Thich Nhat Hanh says, "Every act is a rite." The rite has a beginning, a middle, and an end. See it through.

In zazen, complete your breath-Mu, and then begin the next breath-Mu. If your zazen lacks this kind of distinctness, you are lingering in the dimension of thoughts. They contend with your Mu, and easily overwhelm it.

Notice how you shut the sliding door to the dokusan room. Notice how you make your bows. Do you complete each action?

When one action blurs into the next one, and that one into the next, our lives are deprived of definition, and the inspiration that can only come in the interstices has no chance to slip through.

The Moral Path

1980

The continuing challenge of the Zen student is the integration of his or her practice into everyday life. The most profound truths translate out as honesty with one's self and decency toward others. Realization of the Buddha Way is insight into the emptiness of self-concerns and the oneness of all beings. In daily life this is a matter of ordinary morality.

1982

The Eightfold Path of Right Views, Right Thoughts, Right Speech, Right Conduct, Right Livelihood, Right Effort or Lifestyle, Right Recollection, and Right Meditation was preached by the Buddha to his first five disciplines at Benares, and it remains for us the basic guide for our lives as Buddhists. It begins with Right Views and ends with Right Meditation, but each element of the path depends on all others, so really there is no first step and no last step. The key word is "right," from words in Sanskrit and Chinese that mean "upright, straight, right, correct." Finding what is upright in attitude, thought, speech, action, livelihood, effort, mindfulness, and meditation, and then doing it — this is our life work.

The crisis at Shōbōji in New York [22] serves as an extreme example of the importance of applying our practice. Zazen and the passing of kōans are just cultist tricks unless we carry our quiet, alert, inclusive minds into daily life. There is not one practice in the dōjō and another in the world. The harmony we realize on our cushions is the harmony of social interaction. Forgetting the self in the dokusan room teaches us how to be open to others.

There is no exploitation in the Buddha mind. That is the meaning of the precept, "Don't steal."

1983

I have heard some people say that since Zen says we must be grounded in the place where there is no right and wrong, it follows that Zen has no ethical application. But such logic is very limited. Zen Buddhist experience reveals the harmony and the precious individuality of all beings. If this experience is not applied in the world, then our practice collapses upon itself.

My task and yours, as Yamada Rōshi says, is character perfection. This is the way of realizing self-nature, and the application of that realization lies in the practice of accord in the everyday world.

1985

Antinomianism is the doctrine that true faith gives one freedom from morality. Its expression might be, "Since I am saved, anything goes." This is a heresy that developed early in Christian history, and is particularly associated with the Anabaptists of the sixteenth century.

There is Buddhist antinomianism too. Its expression is "When I am hungry, I eat; when I am tired, I sleep." Yet those same words can also express the highest kind of realization. The Layman P'ang exclaimed, "How miraculous! How miraculous! I draw water! I carry firewood!"[23]

Jukai, the ceremony of accepting the Precepts, is the Zen equivalent to the Refuge Ceremony that is common and fundamental to all forms of Buddhism. In lay Zen centers, including the San'un Zendō, it is offered once a year or so — some people participate each time; some never do. It is not considered a necessary step in the membership or leadership process. People who do take part tend to be those who find a religious base for their zazen, and for their life practice, in ceremonial acknowledgment of their Buddhist heritage. By publicly pronouncing their vows and by wearing the rakusu they are reminded that they wear the Buddha's robes as the Buddha, they eat the Buddha's food, and sleep in the Buddha's bed.

The traditional format of the ceremony does not allow for any individual expression. I would like to work with each participant in advance of the ceremony so that the traditional vows of each can be augmented with personal words of investment. Also, I suggest that we don't need to follow the custom in other Western centers of using Buddhist names socially. It seems rather cultish, somehow. Other minor variations of traditional modes may emerge from our discussions.

1987

In the Purification Gāthā,[24] I repent the bad karma I have created with my body, mouth, and thought. Specifically, what am I confessing? It is useful to know how these categories break down in classical Vinaya:

With my body I have killed, stolen, and misused sex. With my mouth I have spoken falsely, exaggerated, and deceived. With my thought I have been greedy and malicious, and I have belittled.

"I now confess, openly and fully."

1988

At the suggestion of an old-time member, I wish to change one line of our "Purification" gāthā. "Born of my body, mouth, and thought" is the literal translation of the original. It could be helpful to us if this were made interpretive rather than literal and we rendered the line, "Born of my conduct, speech, and thought." This would be a good reminder of Right Speech and Right Action, of Dōgen Zenji's injunction: "Don't permit haphazard speech," and of Sōen Rōshi's caution: "Don't use rootless words."

So let's change it in this way, and apply the message of this more explicit version in our daily lives as well as in our sutra services.[25]

1990

At a recent class devoted to the Precepts, we discussed the possibility of restructuring our program to allow a better integration of the precepts into our everyday practice. Here are some of the points that were raised:

1. As taught in Zen Buddhism, the Buddhist precepts have three aspects: the moral, the compassionate, and the illuminative. However, our spiritual ancestors in Japan tended to depend on Confucianism and the imperatives of monastic life for moral guidelines, rather than on the Buddhist precepts. That left the precepts as kōans, and in all Zen traditions their study was placed at the very end of formal study.

2. When Zen Buddhism moved to the West, Confucianism and the monastery were left behind, and Western students in turn tended to leave their earlier Christian and Judaic teachings of virtues and morality behind as well. This has left a gap in the training of Zen students, whose interests include the application of their practice to daily life.

3. We follow the way of the Bodhisattva as best we can, seeking to integrate our best wisdom with compassion. One way for us to remind ourselves of this Way could be through rituals that encourage us to examine our conduct in light of our vows. We could turn to other Zen centers for models of such rituals, and to other religious traditions as well. Such rituals could supplement the Jukai and Jukai Renewal ceremonies, and help us to internalize the Vinaya, the moral way, which was the first teaching of the Buddha.

Three elements enter into the dynamics of the Sangha. The first is its nature as a family. The second is the need each member feels for personal fulfillment. The third is the imperative of harmony.

These elements are the virtues of the Sangha, and they bring forth its problems. Transference can provide a setting of safety and growth and it can also contribute to dependence. Sibling rivalry can be healthy competition and it can be the source of the most bitter kind of jealousy and conflict.

The Ten Grave Precepts are the guide through this complication, beginning with Not Killing. This is ahimsa, non-harming — giving support and encouragement to others. The other Precepts simply enrich and give detail and explication to the first.[26]

Treat the Precepts seriously and take them to heart. We can then continue to evolve as a harmonious Sangha, with each member on the path to realization.

Yamada Rōshi remarked seven years ago that Zen teachers who exploit their women students lack true realization. Other people have been even more judgmental, accusing Zen practice itself of shortcomings. With more scandals coming to light recently, I have come to understand that both of these criticisms are correct.

Realization means "to make real." Kenshō and kōan study show the insubstantial nature of the self, the joyous harmony of the multi-centered universe, and the precious uniqueness and variety of the many beings. Self-centered conduct obscures these truths, and something has gone dead wrong when a teacher betrays them for his own sexual ends.

You can be sure that Nan-ch'üan and Huang-po never fell into such a pit. Somehow the Buddha Way has become neglected over the generations. Zen teachers must once again make it clear that the Dharma has no power unless it is engaged and used. It is not enough to experience kenshō and study kōans. Insight is only insight, even in the colossal experiences of Wu-men and Hakuin. What those old worthies did with their experiences is what counts. What they did with their daily life practice from their first introduction to the Dharma is what counts. How their characters

evolved is what counts. The gate of transformation is open —
kenshō or no kenshō. Do you walk through or not?

If it is possible for a Zen student to say, "I don't like so-and-
so Sangha member," then it is possible for a Zen teacher to seduce
someone in the dokusan room. Practice has been deliberately set
aside in both cases.

We must return to the Eightfold Path, and not allow it to
remain on paper as just a metaphysical scheme. Right Recollection, which gives rise to all the other steps on the Path, is
aspiration, Bodhichitta, the mind of the Bodhisattva. The student
vows, "I will be a harmonious person, and make all my actions
harmonious. I will respect and cultivate my unique potential, and
give loving encouragement to others to do the same."

We are quick with our strong criticism of Zen teachers who
betray their students and dishonor the Buddha, and it is altogether
right to call a spade a spade in this way. It is also right that we
take ourselves in hand, beginners and old-timers, and cast the
beams from our own eyes.

1991

Most religions use prayer as the way to engage the self with the
highest and best. In Buddhism, the vows fill this function. "I vow
to bring forth my own highest and best." This is Right Recollection, the seventh step on the Eightfold Path.

In the *Hua-yen Sutra* we find the Buddha Maitreya saying: "All
practice derives from vows." Earlier, he praised the pilgrim Sud-
hana, declaring that he had spread a net of vows that pervaded the
universe. In this same sutra we find an entire chapter consisting of
vows in gāthā form.[27] A number of our own sutras are vows, and
in sesshin the Tantō will encourage students to sit down at the
beginning of each period of zazen with a personal vow.

On your cushions you are dealing with the usual human fantasies of sex, personal power, social approval, and wealth. When you look closely, these fantasies are no more than expressions of the Bodhisattva Samantabhadra. Without sex there can be no affection. Without personal power, there is no way you can turn the Dharma wheel. Without social approval, who will listen to you? Without wealth, at least in some degree, you will have no time or energy for zazen. But like sugar in green tea, your fantasies during zazen are not appropriate in the circumstances. They get in the way. Vows can put them in their place.

For example, if one of your fantasies is that you impress people with your wisdom, your vow could be something like "I vow to settle into the place of true wisdom." But such a vow will pop into your head at the right time only if you formulated it earlier. This takes some doing.

It takes a pad and pencil, and a list of your obstacles. With this list complete, write an appropriate vow next to each entry. So "showing off my wisdom" can be accompanied by "I vow to settle into the place of true wisdom." In this way you imprint your vow, and it will occur naturally in your mind when the fantasy comes up. Or when the urge comes up in daily life.

Keep your vows good-humored. Like other aspects of your practice, if your vows are not enjoyable, they will get stale and grim.

Rewrite your list of obstacles and vows as you sense yourself changing and making a ritual of rereading them daily, or weekly. In this way you can spread your own net of vows that pervade the universe, and Samantabhadra can find fulfillment at last.

Unpack karma and you get cause and effect. Unpack cause and effect, and you get affinity. Unpack affinity and you get the tendency to coalesce. Unpack the tendency to coalesce and you get intimacy. Unpack intimacy and you will find that you contain all beings. Unpack containment and there is the Goddess of Mercy herself.

Dreams and Archetypes

1979

All of our ancestors in the Dharma say there is nothing to attain, that the "Dharma King is just this,"[28] and that infinite emptiness is common to all. We call all this the Buddha Tao to give it a name, but names and fine words do not personalize the fact. That only happens when you sit in the dōjō at this breath and you hold the zazen mudrā of your ancestors with your own hands. You personalize their practice as you become absorbed in Mu. You express their teaching in greeting your friends. Just this: no bottom, no limit, nothing to be called the Buddha Tao.

1980

Reading Virginia Woolf's *The Waves* recently, I came across the following:

> [Bernard speaking] "*Everything is strange. Things are huge and very small. The stalks of flowers are thick as oak trees. We are giants lying here, who can make forests quiver.*"[29]

I am reminded of a game I would play in bed when I was very small. I would scratch the sheet, and the sound would be at once tiny and far away, and very loud, close at hand. In zazen, this uncanny condition arises naturally. Your eyes naturally go out of focus and the lens of your cortex likewise goes out of focus. If you give your full attention to Mu in that context, then you are walking near the palace.

Recently a correspondent asked, "Why doesn't Zen speak to the apocalyptic upheavals our planet is undergoing, as Tibetan prophesies do?" I replied that in Zen we seek what underlies and infuses the world of karma and time, including even apocalyptic events, and view the phenomena themselves, as in a dream. Grounded in the dōjō of the Buddha, we live in his dream world. Buddha-nature in personal terms is fundamental rest, fundamental peace. In our dream of apocalyptic upheavals we not only find peace, we practice peace, express peace, present peace, right here in the most miserable karma — not separate from it.

1981

This time I'd like to quote from Kobun Chino Rōshi:

> Student: "What does 'Gaté gaté parasamgaté bodhi svaha' mean?"[30]
>
> Rōshi: "It doesn't mean anything, actually. Everything is falling apart. 'Fall apart, fall apart; all together, fall apart; we can't do anything about it.' That's what 'Gaté gaté' means, really: There is nothing to hang on to.[31]

1982

Recently I have been reading *The Japanese Letters of Lafcadio Hearn*, edited by Elizabeth Bisland. Hearn was a storyteller who lived in rural Japan from 1890 until his death in 1904. His principal correspondent in this collection is Basil Hall Chamberlain, who was Professor of Japanese at Tokyo Imperial University in the same general period. Here is Hearn describing his life with his Japanese wife and their family:

> However intolerable anything else is, at home I enter into my little smiling world of old ways and thoughts and

courtesies where all is soft and gentle as something seen in sleep. It is so soft, so intangibly gentle and lovable and artless, that sometimes it seems a dream only; and then a fear comes that it might vanish away. It becomes Me. When I am pleased, it laughs; when I don't feel jolly, everything is silent. Thus, light and vapory as its force seems, it is a moral force, perpetually appealing to conscience. [32]

What is the appeal to conscience? To belong to the other, as the other belongs to me. To take my turn and laugh when the other is pleased and fall silent when appropriate. To have a role in the vapory, mutual, moral force that is our true home.

Vairochana is the pure and clear Dharmakaya Buddha. In Japan this Buddha is called "Dai Nichi Nyorai, the Great Sun Buddha." Why "Great Sun"?

Huang-po says, "If people would only eliminate all conceptual thought . . . the source substance would manifest like the sun rising in the void and illuminating the whole universe without hindrance or bounds." [33]

As Yün-men said, "What is your light?" Answering for his listeners he then said, "The storeroom, the gate." [34]

1983

The sin of reductionism ranks up there with avarice and lust. It is the black thumb of human cultivation that sears everything it touches. "This very body is the Buddha" becomes "This body is made up of chemicals worth less than twenty-five dollars," or whatever it is.

Reductionism is the way of the cynic who drains life from green leaves and bright flowers until only their shriveled, lifeless forms remain. I want to cultivate poetry, religious experience, naiveté, and love. Your bowls and mine really are the bowls of the Buddha.

1984

Yamada Rōshi had said that hallmarks of the realized person are lightness and briskness. I agree and would add one other: gratitude. Not gratitude toward something, but the spirit of gratitude directed toward everything. The opposite of gratitude is the complaint that life is not fair.

Like briskness and lightness, like zazen, like being decent to others, gratitude can be a practice. Thank you for the leaves, for the cat, for your smile, for your criticism.

What is ritual? It is the instrument of the hidden life. The Buddhas who perform the pageants of enlightenment and its rigors and joys each moment are seen and heard and felt, and their stories become ours as we bow, recite sutras, sit at zazen, walk at kinhin.

Yasutani Rōshi explained makyō as "devil world." I wish I could ask him about this. It seems to me that such an explanation is misleading. I would rather render the word as "uncanny realm." The one who finds himself or herself to be the Buddha, covered with gold leaf or shining light, or who acts out a role in a sacred dream ritual is already on the Buddha's ground, or only needs a step to be there.

1986

Recently, a correspondent suggested that in Zen there is no mystery, and that when mystery is introduced, there is trouble. I agree with what he was trying to say, but I feel that his terminology was not quite right. I would say that in Zen, there must not be mystification, and when mystification is introduced, there is trouble.

Mystery is the unknown in which we live. It is our nature. Mystification is the exploitation of mystery.

1986

Transference is the act of entrusting one's process of growth to another person to some degree. It can be the investment of a lover in a loved one, a student in a teacher, a client in a psychologist, a disciple in a priest. It is an important step in the process of becoming settled in a relationship, becoming educated, and becoming morally and spiritually self-reliant. It has two rules.

The first rule is that each party understand what is happening. Transference is a temporary condition and can lead to a profound relationship that still includes elements of guiding and being guided.

It changes and, with understanding, neither party will give way to the feelings of regret that inevitably accompany the ending of one phase and the beginning of the other. If both parties know in advance that such a period will be difficult, then perhaps it can be met with tolerance and good humor.

The second rule is that neither party betray the process. Responsibility for keeping this rule lies particularly with the one who is trusted, but the one who invests trust also has something to practice. Respect the bond for what it is and don't try to make it something else. In other words, you must not be literal with your affection. I am not really your father; you are not really my children. Transference is a mysterious force. I dream about you, my students — and you dream about me. Transference gone bad has the anguish of divorce and its hatreds. It can destroy lives. Let's be mindful and tender with each other.

1988

Enjoy a samādhi of frolic and play on the sidewalk of birth and death on your way to the temple. Bow in the dōjō with Maitreya and friends and read sutras from maps and calendars. In our midst the Buddha points above and below, announcing his sacred nature and the sacred nature of all beings.

Creation and destruction, form and emptiness, the many and the one: these are the complementarities of the dream. With delight to the depth of tears, we dance our dream.

Time does not pass, but we pass through the evanescent phases of youth, maturity, and old age. If this passage is in the realm of "certain certainties," then the light is hard and glaring. Mu is a device, and realization is reduced to a knack. "I" is either affirmed or denied, and the Dharma remains a convolution of intellectual paradoxes. Finally death is abrupt and agonizing.

The dream's the thing, as well as the play, wherein we'll catch the conscience of the king.

"Every day is a good day," [35] and not only that, every day is joyous. Every day is the Sabbath in the original Hebrew meaning: a day when we celebrate the identity of the other world with this world of change and social interaction.

The ephemeral nature of all beings and all things reveals the essential lightness of the other world that is no other than the one we wake up to each morning. Dukkha, on the other hand, is heaviness, the difficulty of maintaining life against death. Forgetting the self and forgetting time, there is only Kuan-yin answering the telephone with your hands and ears.

Life is too short for all the stuff that just makes it shorter. When the stuff is finally set aside, then life becomes ultimately brief and as open as the sky. What we need is a good sense of proportion. What we need is lightness. What we need is insecurity. What we need is to allow all the sounds to enter.

Recently I had a look at the manuscript of Charlotte Joko Beck's new book, *Everyday Zen*.[36] She has an ABC of practice, standing for "A Bigger Container." What a wonderful expression! Joko doesn't say so, but maybe she would agree that Kuan-yin is the biggest container of all. She hears the whole universe. She contains the whole universe. She accepts all her constituent parts with joy. She accepts each day with joy.

How old is Kanzeon?

1989

At a certain point in the practice, Bodhidharma's response to the Emperor of Liang hits home:

> *The Emperor asked, "Who is this confronting me?"*
> *Bodhidharma said, "I don't know."*[37]

"Knowing is delusion," as Nan-ch'üan said.[38]

How do these messages hit home? I think it happens at the point of hearing, seeing, feeling. To sense something is to forget the self. When you are not sensing, you might respond to a checking question about this case with something like, "When Bodhidharma said 'I don't know,' he knew that he did not know." You would be establishing a position. Bodhidharma had no position.

Bodhidharma did not know and he said so. This is the point of his response. To the very bottom he did not know. "Not knowing is most intimate," Lo-han said.[39] He and Bodhidharma are saying, "Look, I will take you into my confidence. I will show you my heart of hearts. Ready? *I don't know.*"

Of course there are many kinds of knowledge. The knowledge which the old worthies criticized was the knowledge of deconstruction. Not hearing, seeing, sensing, you maintain a firm stance and take their homilies apart. The onion turns out to have no center and you have confirmed your lonely self again.

This is too bad. After all, another term for "not knowing" is "mystery." With Bodhidharma and Lo-han as our teachers, our practice is not to clear up the mystery. It is to reveal the mystery clearly.

One of the workers in our work/training period remarked that our new Zendō building — framed, with the roof sheathed, but by no means finished — already seems old. This sense of the old in practice, pounding nails or breathing Mu, is the dimension of creativity.

It reminds me of an observation made by a woman in a sharing meeting at the Maui Zendō years ago. She said that when she got pregnant she felt in touch with the ancient process of bringing forth life — a process that precedes humanity by millions of years.

So for creativity in zazen we need to be in touch with the very old. We need to escape the time line that puts us in the present with a past in memory and a future in conjecture. On this line we feel as though we were on a train that hurtles us too rapidly past meadows and streams and trees. It does not permit a sense of the ancient at all, but rather insists upon "How I am, how I was, and how I will be."

The woman who experienced the ancient process of procreation as herself had forgotten the self that worries about how *I* come across. Our carpenter member who found she was building an ancient temple was no longer "deluded and preoccupied."[40]

The ancient is the Buddha's dream, the dream of Maudgalayāyana and Shāriputra, the dream of Dōgen and Hakuin, the dream of you and me. Recently in a question period at Koko An, I found myself saying, "You should allow yourself to feel weird." By this I meant that in your zazen you should free yourself from karmic patterns and allow yourself to play in the world where the golden fox chases the silver dog, and to breathe Mu there.

1990

Lately I have been reading *Nature in Asian Traditions of Thought: Essays in Environmental Philosophy.*[41] This is a mixed bag of papers, some of them, it seems, almost deliberately difficult, some of them brilliant. I especially enjoyed the overview, "Pacific Shift," by William Irwin Thompson.

With the "Pacific Shift," Professor Thompson tells us, we enter an era in which the individual is brought back to involvement with the ecology of the whole. Religion itself becomes wholistic — nothing new for Asians, but for the rest of us on the other side of the Pacific, something very new indeed. Truth can no longer be expressed in an ideology, whether that ideology is capitalist, Marxist, Buddhist, or Islamic. Truth is something unnameable that is above or beyond ideology. Technology, which has established the global village, has inadvertently, perhaps, clarified this truth — for one thing, our intimacy with old enemies. We move around with them just as organelles exist symbiotically within the cell.

We are awakening to the great communal world tentatively, still clinging to a substantive psyche, misconstruing our experiences. We isolate ourselves and exploit our environment. The "Pacific Shift" helps us to understand that human maturity is not the individual in control but rather it is fundamental harmony made real.

Thompson quotes from Paul Shepard, author of *Thinking Animals,*[42] to suggest that human thought evolved as the taxonomical array of animals and plants, giving richness of metaphor to the human mind. Thus when species die out, metaphors die with them and no longer inhabit the mind. Our children become mentally handicapped and our species becomes impoverished. Protecting the environment and saving plants and animals is thus more than just avoiding the greenhouse effect. It is preserving human sensibility and the sensibility of the world.

1991

Philip Yampolsky and other scholars are unassailable when they debunk the historicity of the *Platform Sutra* and the Zen Buddhist transmission tables.[43] Bodhidharma, it is clear, never uttered the famous Four Principles, and the Buddha did not twirl a flower before his assembled disciples.[44] All these are dreams, folk stories, mythology.

Our kōan study is intentionally full of nonhistorical stories, from Pai-chang's dialogue with his unevolved self about a fox to Wu-chu's conversation with Mañjushrī about dragons and snakes.[45] Yang-shan dreamed he went to the Tusita Heaven and was led into the presence of the Buddha Maitreya and a vast assembly of noble ones. He delivered a succinct teishō from the third seat and later when he told his teacher Kuei-shan about this experience, Kuei-shan said, "You have attained the level of sage."[46] With his dream, Yang-shan received his teacher's confirmation and confirmation by all the Buddhas.

Transmission is dreamed again when Wu-men reminds us that we "walk hand in hand with all the ancestral teachers in our lineage, seeing with the same eyes, hearing with the same ears."[47] It is dreamed still again when Hsüan-sha says, "The Buddha Shākyamuni and I studied together."[48] And still again in our own transmission and Jukai ceremonies.

It is all a dream. In zazen, the thrush confirms Mu on your cushions. In kinhin, Zen Buddhist students everywhere, past, present, and future, walk mindfully together with us in our dōjō. In sutra services we chant with the Buddha and his disciples down through the ages. When bowing in the dokusan room, you cast everything away as Yamada Rōshi bows before Yasutani Rōshi, as Yasutani Rōshi bows before Harada Rōshi, and so on back — and to come. Interacting in the Sangha, you cultivate your treasure of mutual love and consideration to make this the best possible place to practice. And in your daily life, you recall upon each occasion that all beings are one family, and every one is infinitely precious.

Zen practice is altogether dreary unless it is a celebration of the Buddhas of the Three Worlds and their celebration of us. Post-modernists remind us of relevance — good point! — but when we toss the bath water, Dōgen Zenji remains at the podium. Chao-chou stays too. The Buddha stays. The celebration, difficult and never perfect, is continued endlessly.

One of my colleagues remarked recently, "All is metaphor." It seems to me that this message is the very heart of the Buddha's teaching. When I listen closely to this heart of hearts, I find that I can distinguish three rhythms.

The first rhythm is the natural entropy of human words, concepts, and archetypes. They self-destruct at once because they have no essence. "The Buddha does not have the 32 distinguishing marks of a Buddha," as the *Diamond Sutra* says.[49] There is nothing to believe, there is no ground of faith, the great void itself lies at the heart of expression.

The second rhythm is the power of human words, concepts, and archetypes. The single word Mu has set countless pilgrims on the path of Right Views. "Everyday language is the whole universe," Dōgen Zenji says.[50] "You rice bag!" shouted Yün-men at Tung-shan and Tung-shan was profoundly enlightened and all beings were enlightened.[51] This is the ultimate disclosure, the opening to the universe of the universe.

The third rhythm is the power of notions, concepts, and archetypes expressed by beings of the nonhuman world, with the crack of the clappers at the end of zazen, with the yellow of a field of mustard, with the subtle touch of the wind on wet skin. "When you endeavor in right practice," Dōgen said, "the voices and figures of streams and the sounds and shapes of mountains, together with you, bounteously deliver eighty-four thousand gāthās."[52]

All is metaphor, indeed.

Impermanence

1978

The beginning of the *Hōjōki*, a thirteenth-century Japanese memoir, reads:

> *Ceaselessly the river flows and yet the water is never the same, while in the still pools the shifting foam gathers and is gone, never staying for a moment. Even so is the human being, and human habitation.* [53]

1984

Students at Koko An are expressing the need to slow down and consolidate. We are under a lot of pressure from activities and large numbers of visitors. At the same time, I think we need to look at what underlies the tensions that we feel.

I suggest that, basically, we are all of us conscious of the transitory nature of our lives. Time is passing and we are missing chances for fulfillment. When new responsibilities appear, we resist, feeling that we are not doing justice to our old ones.

Surely all people, not only Zen students, feel this kind of pressure. But there is something unique about the present situation. We sense the transitory nature of our planet. People have faced their own deaths from the beginning of human existence, but never before have men and women had to acknowledge in their hearts that biological evolution as they know it could end.

When we stop to think about it, isn't that what is really troublesome? We go along from day to day, taken up with details of living, but the old purpose of passing along accumulated virtue is missing. We may resist world suicide through peace actions of one sort or another, but what do we do with this tension we feel?

Elsewhere people work with their tensions by building bomb shelters and laying in stocks of food and firearms. We can find this same compulsion in ourselves, in our desire somehow to close our doors a little. I think we need to sort out our feelings.

Our First Vow is to save the many beings. Beneath the tensions of our times, beneath our sense of ephemerality, is nothing, the Buddha nature that is no nature. Once I slept in the same room with a Zen friend who awakened me in the middle of the night, crying out in his sleep, "Vacancy! Vacancy! Wonderful vacancy!" Resting there we can be true to one another, to old friends and new. Renewed there, we can take the peace action that seems appropriate.

In *The Middle Way,* journal of the London Buddhist Society, November 1984, Sōkō Rōshi of Daishu-in remarks:

> *"I feel that the main aim of Buddhism should be to help people to train themselves in their ability to change direction so that they don't think of death as something that comes suddenly at the end of life — as a kind of collapse of the body — but rather that it is in each instant: being born into this situation, dying to that situation, being born into the next situation. If you think in those terms about dying, then each of these instants becomes extremely important."*

We die because we live. We die as we live. To live is to die. It is only by dying to the pretense of life that we can truly live this life of death. Otherwise we live a sham and are undone by the death of a relative or friend, and terrified at the prospect of our own. I revere Tom Issan Dorsey, founder of the Hartford Street Zen Center in San Francisco, who remarked of his illness, "To have AIDS is to be alive."

———

Someone in the early days remarked, "There's always a good movie at the Maui Zendō." Quite apart from what this said about our Sangha, the metaphor of movie for life is an interesting one. The frames go by so quickly that we retain the illusion of continuity and are distracted from the light that shines steadily through each frame.

The metaphor has certain weaknesses, of course, but it helps to show how we are caught by the idea of time. "Tomorrow is another day" — this is a comforting thought when things go wrong, but it cannot be our philosophy of life.

"When can you meet today?"[54]

1987

Yasutani Rōshi lived in a series of little run-down houses he graced with the name "temple." Though he always knew that his stay would be temporary, he would immediately set about repairing faulty doors, broken steps and the like, swinging his own hammer.

We all live in a temporary temple. We honor our heritage by maintaining it as the house of the Buddha.

The Lay Sangha

1978

To use, and not be used by, is the hallmark of the mature Zen person. It is also the hallmark of the mature Zen Sangha. Are we used by our circumstances? Do problems of communication and finances get us down? We take on the coloration of our situation, but unless we are in control it can direct us. The task of the Zen Buddhist Sangha is to see into its situation and find there the basis for effective work.

1979

What is the application of our practice to the administration of our Sangha? How does "body and mind drop away" translate out in matters of building a cottage or planning a sesshin?

Individually, I think it is a matter of focus upon the task, with 100 percent combustion. Collectively, also, it is a matter of focus, with the person chairing the committee and all participants turning the Dharma wheel together.

We aspire to Sangha relations becoming complete[55] and can mark steps in this process with celebrations and festivals. The process itself is the fulfillment, however. If we can forget ourselves in uniting with the task, even little tasks like shopping for sesshin or making out a schedule, then each step can be complete in itself with new intimacy and attainment.

As Zen Buddhism developed in the Far East, compassion became a rather existential concept which was bounded by monastery walls. Also, the emphasis placed upon realization for the individual came to obscure the Buddhahood of all beings.

In the growth of Buddhism in the West, we find there are no monastery walls to limit our suffering with others, and the Sangha is clearly not limited to a sectarian group such as ours. However, we must also break down the personal barriers which divide the "me," so important in Jeffersonian thinking, from true nature. I must acknowledge myself as one being among those who, by nature, are Buddha.

We inherit the Three Jewels — the Buddha, the Dharma, and the Sangha — through a monastic tradition, in which monks and nuns worked out their karma as agents of realization together, quite apart from the dust of the world. We may suppose that today in the West our karma is quite different, since we are a lay society and the dust of the world is part of our daily food.

Yet the monastic model remains an important metaphor. The

Third Jewel in the T'ang period or the twentieth century is the community of practice and the commitment of students to each other. This is not just our refuge — it is the creative center for the Buddha Dharma as we apply it in the larger Sangha of all people, animals, plants, and things.

What is the Sangha? I find myself returning to this question over and over. Some people say the Sangha is everything and every person in the whole universe. This idea is correct, but it can be misused — just as Hakuin's words, "This very body is the Buddha,"[56] can be misused. Personal practice must implement Hakuin's words, and personal investment must implement the universal view of Sangha. Actualizing is our work, individually and socially.

Some people say that Sangha is sanctuary. This idea is correct, but it too can be misused. We need a sanctuary for our zazen, just as we need peace in our hearts individually. But ultimately sanctuary is isolation. I am coming to feel that Buddha Sangha, and by that I mean zendō membership, is a cadre of change. It is a community of people secure in their vision of universal Sangha, grounded in their personal sanctuary, who seek to transmute the poisons of the world in organized and coherent ways.

1982

"Samu" means "work service" — service in the sense of religious service. It is work with hammer and hoe in the same spirit with which sutras are chanted in the dōjō. It is a Sangha experience of temple support, a way to maintain the Dharma that has been a part of Zen tradition for more than a thousand years.

As an expression, "samu" is clarified by the term we have for the walk between our periods of zazen: "kinhin," or "sutra-walk." With this metaphor we can understand that all our everyday actions, walking, sitting, eating, drinking and so on, are actually sutras dedicated to the many beings throughout space and time. We ground ourselves in this understanding in our formal sutra services, as we dedicate these sutras to all beings, all Buddhas.

Our workday here at the temple is a chance to maintain the Buddha Dharma with sutras of cleaning and nailing. We are reminded that our everyday tasks of minding the store and preparing meals are actually sutras of work.

Correction

Early in my Zen training, I was taught that "kinhin" meant "sutra-walk," and indeed this seems to be the usual Japanese interpretation. In the book *Unsui,* for example, it is translated as "sutra going."[57] I have created quite a little folklore on this basis, not only for "kinhin" but also for "samu" — "work service," in the sense of "sutra service."

Thich Nhat Hanh criticizes this interpretation, and says that the "kin" means "passage across," rather than "sutra." I checked in my Chinese-English dictionary, and found both meanings for "kin," and on examining them closely, I am inclined to think he is more right than my Japanese teachers.[58] One of the meanings of "kin," "passage across," is "to experience," and among the compounds under this entry are such terms as "to pass through," "to pass by, undergo" and "to verify." How about "walking verification" as a translation? Keying steps to breath to breath-counting, I verify this very body.

However, we can still find instruction in the interpretations of kinhin as "sutra walk" and samu as "work service."

Zen practice is a vocation, not an avocation. How to work this out in a lay zendō is the ongoing, essentially unsolvable problem that faces us all. We sort ourselves out, on our own, along the scale that ranges from full-time, live-in practice to frequent and then to occasional drop-in participation. Everyone on this scale is welcome, and no invidious comparisons should be made. However, to maintain the Dharma and to convey it to people who seek it, we need a core group of dedicated people who cluster somewhere on the active end of the scale. These are the folks who make a sacred training place possible. These are the folks who make Bodhidharma look profligate.

In Japan, lay Zen is a compromise with the tradition of monasticism, and Right Livelihood is scarcely discussed. For us in the West, however, lay livelihood is the true way. We must establish our own tradition on Shākyamuni's experience under the Bodhi tree and bypass cultural precedent. How does my livelihood teach the Buddha's experience? This is the touchstone.

1983

In the earliest days of the Diamond Sangha, people frequently asked me what I visualized American Zen might be in the future. I would usually evade such questions by stressing the importance of practice in the present. That is well and good, but we must also have an idea of where we are going. Our practice must in a real sense be the practice of our descendants. Somehow we must find the American equivalent of the monastic system, and develop Sangha organization that is participatory and egalitarian within and involved with the broader community outside. We must experiment, use what seems to enhance our practice, take stock periodically to evaluate our direction, test it with the Buddha's own teaching, and then experiment some more. All this takes commitment and flexibility.

The Bodhisattva ideal to save all beings is implicit in the Ten Grave Precepts and in many of our kōans. We need to stress the points that will bring home this aspect in the course of dokusan work, in teishōs and in sharing meetings.

We must be clear that it is possible to have a good experience on the first floor of the psyche, so to speak, while the basement remains full of dust and spiders. Zen experience opens the way to clean up everything from the top to the very bottom, and we should use all expedient means to follow through and expedite this cleanup: diligent zazen, Right Recollection in daily life, and tools such as psychotherapy.

One further point: Our basic practice is zazen. Avalokiteshvara, practicing zazen (deep Prajñā Pāramitā), clearly saw that the way to transform anguish is to realize that forms and our perceptions of them are empty.[59] This teaching reveals the fallacy of relying entirely upon personal thoughts and feelings for guidance. In messy circumstances, full of betrayals and malice, please remember the true self, the empty mind of the universe, so full of rich possibilities. Let's sigh together, acknowledge our weaknesses and flaws and seek the Buddha Tao together, as flexibly, compassionately, and wisely as we can.

1984

January is the time for vows and reevaluation. Anniversaries, such as our twenty-fifth anniversary as a Zendō this year, likewise are times for consolidation and visualization.

Waves from disturbances in other centers are washing our shore and these too remind us that Zen Buddhism is still in the process of acculturation in the West. "Ah, Love, let us be true to one another," Matthew Arnold wrote a hundred years ago, as he sensed the old European culture falling apart. When we are true to each other, then expedient means will appear. We can judge them as good or useless, and practice those that are good.

But if we are not true to each other, then even the cleverest means will break down. Let's remember Arnold's words as our Fifth Vow.

———

The Buddha Shākyamuni recognized the profound difficulty of sound religious practice in the household, and so separated monks and nuns from lay people and established the rule of celibacy for his immediate disciples.

We are faced with the same difficulties of lay practice that Shākyamuni acknowledged. However, the human race is twenty-five hundred years older now. In that long period of time, we can trace a gradual process of encouraging individual responsibility for spiritual growth in world religions. This process has been very uneven, and poisons that infected people in the Buddha's time are now intensified by technology. Nonetheless, I think it is possible to see spiritual self-reliance gradually taking hold in the human mind.

Responsibility for our practice, individually and together, is the only way we can cope with the problems of maintaining true Dharma in a Sangha of householders. Individually, we must find the time for regular zazen, if only three minutes a day. We must take ourselves in hand to practice one-moment Mu between telephone calls, one-moment recollection of our linkage with all beings, one-minute consideration of how the kōan is for me.

At the Zendō, we can understand how the Sangha is the treasure of Buddhism. We polish the Sangha treasure as we practice patience, being true to one another and finding trust and harmony among and within ourselves.

In the Diamond Sangha today, the problems we face arise from the difficulties of lay practice. They are fundamental to what we are. With cool heads and warm hearts we can use these difficulties as the terms of our practice. There is surely no other way.

Trust is the nature of personal practice and of Sangha relations. It is based on the words of Hakuin Zenji, in effect, that all of us are trustworthy.[60] As best we can, we live up to the trust of others and to our trust in ourselves.

Disorganization comes when we stop believing in our own

Buddha nature, our own trustworthiness, and in the Buddha nature of others. That's when we start using excuses. That's when gossip and malicious criticism enter in.

Practice trust.

1985

Musō Kokushi distinguished between three kinds of Zen students: those who shake off entangling circumstances and single-mindedly pursue their practice; those who scatter their attention and are fond of book learning; and those who just repeat the words of old teachers by rote.[61]

This traditional classification was for monks, and it might seem that Musō meant that Zen students should avoid entangling circumstances altogether. But as anyone knows who has lived for a while in a monastery, the circumstances of a monk can include administration, mediation, and community organization. Quite entangling. We shake off confusion by the same means the ancients did, by using circumstances as our terms of life.

These terms include career and family responsibilities. A few minutes of zazen each day, remembering to return to the silence at other times, zazen with others every week or so, a sesshin once a year — these practices can be helpful, but attitude is most helpful of all.

Recently I read an interview in *Zen Ink*, the in-house newsletter of the Zen Center of San Francisco, with Lew Richmond, once designated as next in succession after Reb Anderson by the former abbot of Zen Center, Richard Baker. Lew has left the Center and put off his robes. He is now vice-president of Smith and Hawken, the Mill Valley company that imports fine garden tools. He also pursues his original interest in playing music and composing in his spare time. He continues zazen.

Lew remarks that Suzuki Shunryū Rōshi, the founder of Zen

Center, frequently said that he did not know what he was doing. No one took him seriously, but, Lew says, he really did not know what he was doing. Suzuki Rōshi was being very honest, but perhaps he did not make his point forcefully enough, so people depended on what they thought was his wisdom when he made suggestions.

Reading Lew's words I am reminded that I probably do not set forth my own uncertainties emphatically enough. I have clear ideas about the importance of zazen and the development of realization and mindfulness, and about the importance of using skillful means that will keep us on the path, individually and as a Sangha. However, I don't always see clearly what those means should be. I want to experiment together with each of you, and together with the Sangha collectively, to establish skillful means, and to keep communication open in judging them.

During our recent orientation workshop someone asked me, "In transmitting Zen Buddhism to the West, what is essential to retain?"

I replied, "Zazen."

The questioner continued, "Is there any other essential element?"

I replied, "No."

There is, of course, no zazen without people, and people find it useful to build shelter, develop procedures, and cultivate a particular style. We can vary our shelter, procedures and style as we like. The very name of our practice, however, is Zen (Meditation). There is no Zen without Zen.

1991

Recent sharing meetings have brought forth divergent views about the Sangha, its rationale and its goals. These discussions have helped me to see the issues more clearly, and I am grateful to the facilitators and to the participants. I am stimulated to formulate my own views.

1. It seems to me that the joy of practice is forgetting the self in the act of uniting with something — to paraphrase our old teacher, Yamada Rōshi. This is surely true informally everywhere, as well as on our cushions in the dōjō. Likewise the joy of community is in the common task — in our case, to clarify the Way of the Buddha and to create its best possible setting.

2. We should not hurry to acculturate. It took eight generations — from Bodhidharma to Ma-tsu and Yüeh-shan — for Dhyāna Buddhism to become truly Chinese. Like our ancestors, however, we should be alert to those possibilities of change which are in the spirit of the teaching.

3. To extend that second point: we work out our innovations as Zen Buddhists, not just as Zen students. We are late-twentieth-century Americans, and at the same time and in this very place we find ourselves in the dreams of Shākyamuni, Ananda, Chao-chou, Dōgen, and our own Yamada Rōshi. Like the family and friends of Black Elk reenacting his profound vision of horsemen from the four directions, we reenact the dhyāna of the Buddha and his disciples in their monsoon retreats, right here at Koko An. I bow in veneration to the most exalted one.

4. Tension can be healthy or unhealthy. We all know about unhealthy tension. It keeps us awake at night. Healthy tension is the natural complementarity of structure and inspiration, responsibility and personal fulfillment, discipline and freedom, authority and egalitarianism, tradition and relevance, male and female, form and the void, life and nonexistence. Neglect one side of the pair, and it will turn around and bite.

5. Finally, all of us have our personal problems. I am inspired by Te-shan and more recent teachers who transformed their personal qualities from neuroses to virtues. This transformation is my responsibility for myself; your responsibility for yourself. However, we can help each other. Let me know when something is off and I will do likewise for you. This is the gift, constantly circulating and enriching the world.

Recently I asked Sulak Sivaraksa, the Thai Buddhist activist, "Generally in the United States these days, husband and wife both work. They are tired when they get home and must look after their children and their house. They scarcely have energy for coming to a Buddhist meeting, much less for engagement in the community. What suggestions do you have for this dilemma?"

He answered graciously and gently, acknowledging the problem, pointing out that it is not just a matter of budgeting time and energy. It is, he said in effect, a matter of life-style.

In other words, the nice house and nice car and the private school are the problem. They need protection and maintenance. They focus our attention upon the unit, rather than upon the whole. Society itself, as we have structured it, needs protection and maintenance too; the cost is felt by everyone and ordinary folks must exhaust themselves just to put food on the table.

This is Wrong Effort, somehow. Right Effort, on the other hand, is Right Life-style and indeed this is the Chinese understanding of the term: the Way of the Sage, living on the plainest of food in the plainest of accommodations.

Yet following the Way of the Sage individually would itself be isolative. Somehow we must conspire together in networks to build the Buddha's way of interdependence within and beside the acquisitive system that is all about us, using the tools and lines of communication that are already in place for our own global purposes. Otherwise we are maintaining a steady course of using up ourselves and the world.

Kōan Study and Its Implications

1981

One of the participants at the recent conference on Dōgen Zenji at Tassajara was Hee-Jin Kim, Professor of Religion at the University of Oregon. Author of the cogent, scholarly *Dōgen Kigen: Mystical Realist,* Dr. Kim read a paper called "Method and Realization: Dōgen's Use of the Kōan Language."[62] In this paper he casts a critical eye on D. T. Suzuki's treatment of kōan language as a means rather than as a presentation.

Dr. Suzuki regarded the kōan as a paradox which entices the student to seek a solution. This search leads to a blank wall which must be broken through by sheer force of will and spirit.

On the other hand, Dōgen Zenji says, "Discriminating *is* words and phrases, and words and phrases *liberate* discriminating thought." Dr. Kim goes on to say, "In other words, the kōan language presents the workings of Buddha Nature."[63]

This reminds me of Seikan Hasegawa's definition of a kōan, "A matter to be made clear."[64] The Tao is not a matter of deliberate frustration and release. It is a matter of becoming intimate with, say, Mu. Mu presents the workings of Buddha nature. It is not a device to force you into a corner.

1988

Kōan study is the practice of the Buddha Way, as set forth by Dōgen Zenji:

> To study the Way of the Buddha is to study the self. To study the self is to forget the self; to forget the self is to be confirmed by the ten thousand things. To be confirmed by the ten thousand things is the dropping away of body and

mind, and the body and mind of others. No trace of real-ization remains, and this no-trace is continued endlessly. [65]

What was called the self, growing up from childhood, turns out to be the skin of isolation. It sloughs off and is forgotten when the song of a cardinal emerges as one's own consciousness, when the laugh of a child emerges, when the pain of a friend emerges. The fact that "I am large — I contain multitudes" becomes clear, and then more clear, for me and for everyone.

Each point in this clarification is a peak experience, and is only a glimpse at best. Even the Buddha's realization under the Bodhi tree was a glimpse, a very deep and broad glimpse, of course, but one which he could make more and more clear for himself and others thereafter through his long life of practice and teaching. Unless you take yourself in hand like the Buddha and take up the practice of clarifying more and more deeply the many implications of your realization, the cardinal singing with your own voice becomes no more than a memory, and the way opened by that realization is obscured.

These days, I am hearing that kōan study is framed in a cultural context that is far away and long ago, that it is not relevant to our times. The samurai in Kamakura made the same complaint to their Chinese teachers, so those teachers made very sincere efforts to Japanize the teaching. You can read about their work in Trevor Leggett's books — full of kōans with a Japanese flavor.[66] However, few of those acculturated kōans survived. Our own kōan curriculum is derived from Japanese teachers, but only "The Sea of Isé" remains from the effort to make the study familiar to Japanese students:

> *In the Sea of Isé,*
> *ten thousand feet down,*
> *lies a single stone.*
> *I wish to pick up that stone*
> *without wetting my hands.* [67]

The one Japanese element here is the place-name. Likewise there are certain Chinese historical, geographical, and folkloric elements in kōan study, but these are easily explained. The kōans themselves arose in T'ang times, an extraordinary period of cultural efflorescence where culture itself was transcended. These are family jewels and we reset them only with the utmost care.

More about Zen study and relevance: I'm told that lay people don't have time to practice. My own life is very busy and I have a real problem budgeting my time, so I can understand this difficulty. Still, with half an hour per day of zazen at home and a Sunday morning at the Zendō, one can maintain the practice. I suggest that the real problem is not lack of time, or irrelevance of kōans to the modern world. Rather it is, so to speak, the irrelevance of the modern world to Zen practice. The problem is with livelihood itself. How can the Zen student earn a living and raise children in the context of an acquisitive society? In that context, it is difficult to keep intimate with others. This is our dilemma.

I have long felt that the Catholic Worker movement offers a model to modern, Western Buddhists as the Sangha for our time. This is a network of autonomous households of nuclear or extended families, practicing a common Dharma, offering mutual support within the family, within the network and within the larger community. In such a setting one can conspire with friends to earn food, clothing, bedding, and medicine and at the same time offer a hand to others — ultimately, one hopes, helping them to slough away limited views.

Catholic Workers speak of themselves as anarchists but they do so with a smile. The anarchist worthy of the name is one who takes responsibility for the truth, and joins with people of like minds for the strength required to fulfill the truth in daily life — without any sort of exclusiveness or isolation. The Wobblies called this "building the new within the shell of the old."

1989

It has been interesting to hear the responses to my recent words about kōan study and the relevance of Zen practice. People either loved them or hated them, it seems. I myself feel that I probably oversimplified.

Zazen and kōan study provide a medium for realizing the other person, animal, or plant as an avatar of the mystery. But there is more. The practice is like the tail of the buffalo that never completely passes through the window. It is available for people who simply must practice.

In the old days, taking the Buddha's path meant abandoning everything and going to the forest but today the forest is not an option. We must leave home without leaving home. How to do this is our basic problem.

I think leaving home without leaving home means avoiding the poisons and not encouraging them in our livelihood or life-style — easier said than done. We can build upon our Sunday programs and integrate families fully into our Zen work, but if our lives in the world do not reflect what we learn in kōans, in the Precepts, and in the Pāramitās — if our lives don't reflect the integration we find in zazen, then we will be just a cult that is divided off from the world. Somehow we must face the systemic delusions that feed upon themselves and threaten all life. We must then establish our place as Zen students in the context of all that corruption. I am inspired by the Catholic Worker, but burnout and self-righteousness are problems found here and there in that movement. We can draw on our own heritage of wisdom and compassion to be patient with each other and find our path.

A correspondent recently asked me whether or not I believe in karma. I replied that I do not, any more than I believe in gravity. The question is faulty. It posits karma as a thing or maybe even as a kind of deity. "Karma" simply means "action," and the reason of action: affinity and causation.

The most profound fact described by the word "karma" is mutual inclusion — "interbeing," to use Thich Nhat Hanh's term. I include you and all beings; you include me and all beings. Each of us is unique and precious and we are individually the universe in a particular guise. Anything that happens to any of us happens to all. If I resist this natural law, then I create disharmony throughout the limitless organism. When I work toward clarifying interbeing, then I am turning the Wheel of the Dharma by whatever name.

The organism is the Sangha, the big Sangha of the fathomless universe, the medium Sanghas of various dimensions, cosmic and mundane, and tiny Sanghas made up of only a few members in the most microscopic particle. The Buddha Sangha is one such organism. Mahayana, Theravada, and Vajrayana are akin and each of their many branches has its own familiar intimacy. Enhancing these affinities is our karma, our work.

Understanding karma, standing under the term and making it my own, is to become its meaning and to give personal energy to the great rotation. Be clear about this. Taking the Buddha's word into ourselves so completely in daily life that there is no residue — this fulfills his vows forever.

1990

What is my main purpose in a Sangha meeting? — that my particular point of view should prevail? — or that the Sangha should be allowed to evolve with my input in a mix with those of others? The two options are very different.

If my purpose is to get my point of view accepted and put into practice, then I will come to the meeting with fixed intentions, and no process will be possible. I might even get mad when things don't go my way and drop out of the program completely. This has happened in the past in our own Sangha.

In other organizations, the conviction that my way is absolutely right can lead to the parliamentary conspiracy. Three or four of us get together and agree: "You make the motion, I second it, then you make the point vigorously in the discussion, I call for the motion before anyone else can speak, you second it, and we vote it through." This is called railroading, and legislatures, labor unions, and businesses use it as a matter of course. Fortunately our style of decision-making by consensus limits this kind of insensitive domination of the group.

It comes down to practice, and practice, after all, is conduct in keeping with Right Views. Of course, Right Views are not merely opinions, not even Skākyamuni's opinions, but are views that accord with this realization: we are all in this together and we aren't here very long. Let's take care of one another while we can.

Integrity and Nobility

1982

One of our ancestors in the Dharma, not the Zen Buddhist Dharma but the Big Dharma, is Mahatma Gandhi. He lived by Satyagraha, a word he coined from Hindi, which means "holding to the truth." Gandhi held to the truth in his long campaign for India's independence from British rule — we can do the same in our own long campaigns.

I don't know who it was that said "Every man has his price." Some forgettable person. Living by Satyagraha you have no price. Your integrity can't be compromised. You don't play games now so that you can be straight later.

Reflecting on the young men who died recently in the freezing water of the South Atlantic and on the families who are dying now in the rubble of ruined buildings in Beirut, I am reminded again of the inexorable workings of karma. The Israeli-Palestinian conflict has roots in the holocaust in Germany and Poland, which has roots in the defeat of Germany in World War I, which has roots . . .

Karma is relatively easy to explicate in detail when it happens out there, in world affairs. The issues are quite clear-cut. Violence leads to violence, and we need to awaken ourselves and others to the importance of peace as our life-style and livelihood.

It is also important that we find this way in our individual lives together in the Sangha, in our families and among our colleagues and friends. Moreover, Satyagraha, is not just a device or technique to be taken up or set aside, depending on the circumstances. I suggest that so-called pragmatic behavior, another term for a conspiracy of greed, has no place in our lives as Zen Buddhists. It is not necessary to isolate ourselves as saints but it is important to find skillful means to live the truth.

1984

We devaluate ourselves and neglect our potential if we permit ourselves to indulge in gossip and foolish talk. Time is passing. You and I are not Shākyamuni, but we can practice our own best potential, and thus express the Buddha's mind fully and completely at each step on the path.

1988

In putting away my books the other day, I ran across a volume of poetry with my grandmother's signature on the flyleaf: Jessie Louise Thomas. It was dated 1879, when she was twelve years old. Above her name, in faint pencil, she had written:

> *Better not be at all*
> *Than not be noble.*
> — Tennyson

Values like nobility, merit, and even morality have unfortunate overtones of hypocrisy these days, but this does not diminish their perennial virtue. My grandmother aspired to nobility from her Victorian childhood, and she raised her own children and influenced her grandchildren to be noble. She knew nothing of the Buddha, but echoed his words: "Be upright in your views, in your thoughts, in your speech . . ."

Noble, upright speech arises from clear understanding that none of us will be here very long and it behooves us to be kind to one another while we can. It arises from knowing in our hearts that we need each other and cannot survive alone. I vow to speak out of consideration for the frailty of my friends, and my own frailty, and out of consideration for our intimate family relationship. I vow not to speak as though the errors of others were ingrained or as though I were separate.

I vow to live up to my grandmother's aspiration and to the Noble Path of the Buddha.

We discussed *kshānti*, or patience, last month during our classes on the Pāramitās, so recently I was interested to come across the transcription of a talk by the late Nechung Rinpoché that touched on the same subject. "Patience is a pass," Rinpoché said. The ordinary pass is a piece of paper that can be misplaced or destroyed. Don't lose your pass of patience.[68]

As a Tibetan who lived as a refugee in India and as an immigrant to the United States, Nechung Rinpoché knew that the pass is the skillful means of reconciliation. With a pass, all barriers are leveled.

"Harmony is important," Rinpoché said by way of introducing his topic. Indeed, the nature of the Sangha is harmony, not just the Buddhist community, but also the family, the nation, and the world — including animals, plants, and things. It is with patience that harmony is realized and manifested.

"Don't keep your pass of patience in your pocket," Rinpoché said. "When you get an angry look, show your pass." This is the

Kshānti Pāramitā, the way of personal fulfillment that is also universal fulfillment.

On reading Philip Sherrard's *The Eclipse of Man and Nature*,[69] I was struck by his suggestion that every religious person is a priest. This is in keeping with my injunction during sesshin that every participant is a leader, but my words simply refer to the manner of the student in the dōjō. Sherrard's point is deeper, and as a theme for the Diamond Sangha it is particularly interesting.

In our dōjō, every person is lay. In a sense this is the same as "every person is a priest." We do not have a hierarchy of ordained over non-ordained. But just as "everyone is a leader" encourages people to take responsibility for sesshin, so "every person is a priest" deepens my awareness and yours of the religious responsibility implicit in our status.

Religious responsibility will be different for each individual, but the Sixteen Bodhisattva Precepts are excellent guidelines.

1990

There is not much nobility in the pursuit of comfort and convenience — for example the comfort and convenience of air conditioning. The pursuit of comfort and convenience involves the imperative to protect the systems that support an easy life, and eventually we find ourselves in a most uneasy position indeed. Convenience at the expense of others is greed, and its protection ultimately leads to war. Recent events in the Middle East expose the bellicose greed of convenience in a most naked manner. Now we can see clearly into the vanity of "national self-interest" and "protecting our way of life." What is our self-interest, after all, but that of everyone and everything!

The Buddha advised his followers to leave the life of comfort and convenience. This was his way of spreading comfort and convenience to all beings. When there is less for me, there is more for the multi-centered me that pops up everywhere across the world. On the other hand, when there is more for me, then there is less for the multi-centered me, and children die, forty thousand of them every day from malnutrition. The universe cannot remain unbalanced in such a way. What goes around comes around and then behind our stone walls topped with broken glass we get it in the neck.

Now we are faced with an extremity — another war in the Third World, maybe the third big one of this century. We are like people in a little boat in high seas, acknowledging that we should never have made this trip. It is time to calm the waters as well as we can with our words and actions. It is time to reach out and work with our friends.

The Net of Indra

1982

When Gary Snyder read his poetry in San Francisco recently, he began by asking members of the audience to enjoy their breathing and then he said, "Thich Nhat Hanh taught me that." Thich Nhat Hanh was next on the program and before he read his poems he said to the audience, "Enjoy your breathing." Then he added, "Gary Snyder taught me that."

The audience enjoyed a good laugh, but I wonder if everybody truly saw the point of the joke. In our con-spiracy, we enjoy our breathing together, mutually interacting — and really, is there anyone who is not a teacher? Anyone who is not a student?

1983

"Attachment" is a term often misunderstood by people who are beginning Zen practice. "I must not be attached," they think. I knew a woman who gave away her three-year-old child for that reason. People preoccupied with non-attachment are incapable of love.

Actually, everything is attached to everything else. Kenshō is a realization that the sound of the little stream is not separate from myself. "Non-attachment," to use the term correctly, is the content of this experience: the stream, the sound, are already elements of me. I need not concern myself about attachment to them or about non-attachment from them. Unless attachment and non-attachment are understood positively in this way, the path is missed.

1986

The *Hua-yen Sutra* presents the doctrine of interpenetration: I and all beings perfectly reflect all people, animals and plants.[70] The metaphor is the "Net of Indra," the last great development in Mahayana thinking. It is a model of the universe, in which each knot of the net is a jewel that perfectly reflects all the other jewels. This model is made intimate in Zen study, beginning with our examination of the Buddha's own experience on seeing the Morning Star, when he exclaimed, "I and all beings have at this moment attained the Way."[71]

In our mealtime sutra we acknowledge the perfect reflection: "First we consider in detail the merit of this food and remember how it came to us."[72] We tend to recite this line mechanically, yet it is a clue for the practice of the Net of Indra in daily life.

Where did this tomato grow? Who were the farm workers?

Who were their family members? Where did their seeds come from?

I bow in gratitude.

1988

You marvel that this matter, shuffled pell-mell at the whim of Chance, could have made a man, seeing that so much was needed for the construction of his being. But you must realize that a hundred million times this matter, on the way to human shape, has been stopped to form now a stone, now lead, now coral, now a flower, now a comet; and all because of more or fewer elements that were or were not necessary for designing a man. Little wonder if, within an infinite quantity of matter that ceaselessly changes and stirs, the few animals, vegetables, and minerals we see should happen to be made; no more wonder than getting a royal pair in a hundred casts of the dice. Indeed it is equally impossible for all this stirring not to lead to something; and yet this something will always be wondered at by some blockhead who will never realize how small a change would have made it into something else.

— Cyrano de Bergerac
Voyage de la lune, 1661

This remarkable passage, prefiguring Buddhist teaching for the Western mind, is translated and quoted by Italo Calvino in his posthumous *Six Memos for the Next Millennium.*[73] Calvino goes on to show that Cyrano understood how the workings of Chance with common stuff proclaims the kinship of all beings. He imagines the protest of a cabbage about to be beheaded:

*Man, my dear brother, what have I done to you to deserve
death? . . . I rise from the earth, I blossom forth, I stretch
out my arms to you, I offer you my children as seed; and
as a reward for my courtesy, you have my head cut off.*

Most Western people consider Confucianism to be moral philos-
ophy, but it is more. It is, in fact, one of the parents of Zen
Buddhism. In a recent essay, "The Continuity of Being: Chinese
Visions of Nature,"[74] Professor Tu Wei-ming sets forth the
Confucian view of the universe as a single body whose moving
power is *ch'i*, pure and penetrating, yet not discernable in form.
This cosmic function is impersonal and impartial. Each being is
its modality in a particular form and activity.

All modalities are made of "ch'i," and thus human beings are
organically related to rocks, trees, and animals. Professor Tu calls
this view "moral ecology," and quotes the Confucian writer
Chang Tsai: "All people are my brothers and sisters, and all things
are my companions."

Ch'i runs creatively through sisters, brothers, and companions
that make up the universe. Exchange and interplay among the
many forms and species are altogether possible, and this transformative option has an important place in Chinese literature. In
Monkey, the hero is born from a piece of agate, and in *The Dream
of the Red Chamber*, Pao-yü is transformed from a piece of jade.
The heroine of the *Romance of the White Snake* develops the power
to transfigure herself into a human being in the course of several
hundred years of self-cultivation.

There are profound implications for zazen here. The word *ch'i*
can enrich our understanding of Essential Nature, a term that
sometimes seems rather static. In everyday Chinese, *ch'i* is the
word for "breath," a word whose English etymology is "welling
up." Life welling up is, for the Chinese, life in constant transformation. Thus your breath is none other than the transformative
power of the universe. Let Mu breathe Mu, and you are putting
yourself in harmony with your sisters and brothers as they evolve

themselves, and with your companions the moon, the planets, and the stars in their awesome, unknown destiny.

Nonviolence within the Zendō and Outside

1979

Our month of intensive training at Koko An this month coincides with a conference and a court case relating to nuclear weapons. This coincidence in time can be an occasion for us to examine the role of the Zen student in dealing with the murderous violence implicit in the preparation for war.

The nation-state and the multinational corporation, by and large, are giant conspiracies of exploitation. Their vitality depends upon acquisition, and their technology has brought the world to the very point of conflict in their competition. The nature of the conflict would be such that, for example, our State of Hawaii might be laid waste.

Yet it is clear that opposition, even successful opposition, plays the same poisonous game. Opposition to President Johnson led to the election of President Nixon, opposition to the B-1 Bomber led to the Cruise Missile. Opposition to Waikele Gulch led to West Loch.[75] The juggernaut can be diverted, but is difficult to transform.

We are critical of Marxists for alleging that the end justifies the means and yet we hold demonstrations as though we were in the Marxist camp. We do not know, really, what will happen in the future. We cannot be successful in achieving any particular end. Eternity is in this very *nen*, this very thought-moment. Let us celebrate eternity with the theatre which truly presents it.

1982

"Takuhatsu" is the term for the practice of monks and nuns walking the streets of cities and towns, chanting sutras and accepting offers of money or rice for temple support.

When I see takuhatsu on the streets of Kamakura or Tokyo, I have a strong sense of the ancient. Ragged monks in archaic bamboo hats thread their way through well-dressed commuters in a setting of trains, trucks, buses, taxis, and commercial buildings. I am reminded not of some hidden truth, but of something lost, or almost lost, in the passage of time.

What is our takuhatsu as Western Zen students? A Zen journal is an obvious analogy: teaching, and, we hope, raising money. There are other analogies, such as orientation programs, and the occasional university class presentation. The Buddha Sangha also has a role in the larger Sangha, with Christian, Jewish, and humanist friends, to encourage social justice, peace, and the protection of animals and plants.

Zen Buddhism has declined in Japan, probably because it has remained within the monastery, emerging for the most part only in activities that accord with government and business policies. It seems to me that our journals and our appearances as Zen Buddhists outside the Zendō must be in support of our temple Earth, as well as our place of formal practice.

What, sensible people may ask, are you doing sitting there on your butt in the presence of some three thousand nuclear weapons stored just a few miles away? Our takuhatsu will be organic when it nourishes peace in that dimension as well as within the dōjō.

1983

My words on these pages relate to Zen practice as a rule, but coming out of sesshin and reading about the invasion of Grenada, I find that I am thinking about American foreign policy more than about encouraging people to pay attention to their spiritual purpose. I suggest that all of us inform ourselves about Grenada, beginning with the fact that it is smaller than the island of Lanai, and then write about it, to newspapers, to friends, to congresspeople. The situation is so bizarre — so likely to trigger a larger conflagration — that somebody must speak out and say how grotesque it really is. This is one way we can use the energy of innocence we cultivate during sesshin.

At a recent class I said that it is better to question than to affirm when teaching, since the question can bring forth responses that are already at least partly formed in the minds of others and the teacher will not be imposing her or his views. This point needs to be qualified, of course. Not all questions are really questions. If you are a teacher, can you ask your question without imposing a view?

1989

I had the pleasure of meeting with Joanna Macy recently, and she shared with me a communication she had sent to colleagues in preparation for a panel discussion being planned around the forthcoming visit of the Dalai Lama to the San Francisco Bay Area. Here are ideas I have lifted from that communication.

Joanna points out that we live in a world that can die. Whole species and life-support systems are already dying, and massive want, hunger, oppression, disease, and conflict assail a growing proportion of the planet's beings. We can do something about it and yet we tend to act as if we don't believe what is happening. She asks, "How can we become simply *present* to what is going on and let it become real to us? Great adventures await us; what is it that erodes our will, our creativity, our solidarity?"

Joanna finds that many people (especially those drawn to Eastern paths) have developed notions about spirituality which hinder them from realizing their power to effect change. Among the "spiritual traps" which cut the nerve of compassionate action are these:

1. That the phenomenal world of beings is not real. With this view the pain of others and the demands on us which are implicit in that pain are less tangible than the pleasures or aloofness we can find in transcending them.

2. That any pain we may experience in beholding the world derives from our own cravings and attachments. With this view, the ideal way to deal with suffering becomes non-attachment to the fate of all beings, not just non-attachment to matters of the ego.

3. That we are constantly creating our world unilaterally through our subjective thoughts. Confrontation is considered negative thinking, acceptance is positive. Therefore it is concluded that when we confront the injustice and dangers of our world we are simply creating more conflict and misunderstanding.

4. And the corollary, that the world is already perfect when we view it spiritually. We feel so peaceful that the world itself will become peaceful without our need to act.

Shackles and traps drop away in such lucid exposition of Wrong Views. Our responsibilities stand forth clearly.

1990

I have been thinking about nonviolence from the Buddhist perspective recently. It seems to me that it follows on the Eightfold Path very neatly.

Right Views, the first step on the Path, reveal a world in which beings are in constant flux, coming into life and passing away. These beings are in symbiosis, with everything depending intimately on everything else. This intimacy is more than closeness; everything is inherent in everything else. I include all things — multitudes, as Whitman says.

Yet each being is unique. Each element of each being is unique. Each leaf of each tree has its own special form. This is the marvelous dynamism of the universe. The function of each individual is to mature as a unique entity with the clearest awareness possible that my fulfillment is the fulfillment of all and the fulfillment of each other being is the fulfillment of all.

Nonviolence is the Tao of such fulfillment. Violence to another is violence to all, including myself. Very simple to say; very difficult to practice.

1991

I have just finished reading William Jordan's *Divorce among the Gulls*.[76] It is deceptively simple sociobiology that has profound implications for the human race and all species at our time of great crisis.

Jordan points out that the smallest increment that fossil record can resolve is about 100,000 years. Things that happen within that length of time can't be separated and identified.[77] So project yourself ahead 70 million years. That's the time that has passed since the age of the dinosaurs. You come upon fossils of *Homo sapiens.* You won't be able to tell which came first, the Neanderthal or the atomic age. You won't know whether the Buddha Shākyamuni came before or after the computer.

Thus, in units of Earth time, all of human civilization has arisen like a flash, like a nuclear explosion. So the question Jordan raises is, "How do you control a flash?" A greenhouse effect has developed in the past hundred years, a hole in the ozone layer appeared in the past thirty years, three billion people have been added to the world population since 1950. The current destruction of the environment will, in the distant future, be indistinguishable from the impact of an asteroid.[78]

This is, as Jordan says, philosophical hardball. Is the human mind any more capable of controlling its destiny than those giant lizards who died out 70 million years ago? Think of this, he suggests, as you turn the ignition key of your car and send gasoline through its veins — gasoline, a liquid extracted from the bodies of the dinosaurs and their habitat.

As we face a full-blown ground war in the Persian Gulf, it becomes clear that human beings and other beings are being sacrificed for that ancient lizard juice and for its temporary power. Events seem to be accelerating even the flash.

Well, maybe paleontologists can't distinguish the conduct of beings from millennium to millennium, but students of the mind can see the passage of one thought to the next and switch readily from the lizard mind to the mind of the Bodhisattva. The answer to Jordan's hard question is *yes* — with the power of the Bodhisattva we can control human destiny and the destiny of the Earth, *if we will*. We can conspire with like-minded friends to shut off the gas and oil of the powers of annihilation. This would be conservative action, taken from the conservative position of our First Vow.

About Practice

1977

Question: "I got your tape today and found it most interesting. However, as I am in prison, I have no funds to pay for books. Is there a way you can help me?

"I find the breath-counting very relaxing. I have had no problem with this as yet, except when I sit with my legs in my lap for a long time. I have trouble walking afterwards. Is there something I am doing wrong? I'll close for now. Peace be with you."

Response: "I'm sending you my collection of orientation talks. I hope you find it useful. About your practice — it is good that you can find breath-counting to be relaxing. This shows that you are doing it correctly. Sink into the count. Melt into the count. On the first breath, there is the first thought. Let that breath and that thought be 'one.' On the next breath there is the next thought. Let that breath and that thought be 'two.' Not two things, just the number 'two.' Then the next breath and thought is 'three' and so on up to 'ten,' and up to 'ten' again, and again. But don't be too concerned about reaching 'ten.' Let there be only the number, and all around it there is nothing, just silence and space. Only 'one,' only 'two,' only 'three,' and so on. In this way, you find true rest, true peace.

"It is natural that your legs go to sleep. If you limit your periods of sitting to twenty-five minutes, then you cannot harm yourself by sitting in half-lotus, unless you are unusually stiff, or already have an injury or have some other physical handicap such as arthritis. Be sure, however, that you are quite flexible before attempting full-lotus (both feet in the lap). It is definitely possible to injure your knee or your hip by attempting full-lotus too soon, so go easy and do just a little at a time.

"Do stretching exercises as well as zazen. Stretch muscles and tendons in your groin, thighs, knees, and ankles. When you do zazen, your two knees and your rear end form a triangle. Your rear end should be elevated a few inches above the level of your knees. In this way you can keep your back comfortably straight. Keep your head up and your eyes lowered. When it comes time to stand, take it easy. Take hold of your ankle and knee, lift your leg, and let it down to the mat. Stand slowly with your feet on a hard surface and wait a bit before you step out. Your circulation will return soon.

"All of us here join in sending you loving good wishes for

peaceful and fruitful zazen. Take good care of yourself physically — your health is very important. Some teachers say you should ignore the self, but your self is the agent of peace and realization. Please be careful with it."

1979

Do you deplore waste? Live by cultivating. Cultivating begins with the agent of realization, the one drawing this breath. Use this breath.

Do you deplore violence? Live by nurturing. Nurturing begins with this spoon or with this friend. Take care of your spoon. Take care of your friend.

Thus you ground yourself in awareness and compassion. Decisions about Right Livelihood and social action arise here.

1981

There are two questions before the Zen student: "How do I do it?" and "How do I apply it?"

These two questions run together. One applies it by doing it. Attention on the cushions naturally leads to attention in daily life. The more practice each day, the better the attention on and off the cushions. In concrete terms, this means not letting a day go by without zazen. Where you can, conspire with family members and friends to keep a schedule.

But, you may ask, how does all this lead to compassion? Attention is compassion. When someone asked me, "How may I save all beings?" I replied, "By including them." Attention is not separation, but inclusion. Include Mu, include griffins when they are the subject of your attention, include other people when you say hello.

———

You can rhapsodize about wise words of the old teachers and speculate about the meaning of the Dharma but you miss the central purpose of your practice.

You must cut off the mind road, as Wu-men said. That is, you must cut the tape which plays and replays the old drearies.

Wu-men wrote:

> *If you argue right and wrong*
> *You are a person of right and wrong.*[79]

When your eye is upon joy and misery, you are a person of joy and misery. When your eye is upon realization and ignorance, you are a person of realization and ignorance. But when you see clearly that all these concepts are transparent, with nothing to them at all, then you are a person of torch ginger.

1982

The dross of our lives is the residue of old greed and self-centeredness which we have carried over from days before we began the practice. Momentarily we forget how to listen. Momentarily we forget the integrity of others. Momentarily we permit concepts to become absolute. These moments of dross tie into each other, and we can find ourselves superficially motivated.

With the Mu-sigh that punctuates the day of a Zen student, it is good also to remember the "Great Vows for All," and put them into practice.

Human beings tend to gather in groups and to share certain concepts within those groups. This is all right; I too prefer to be with people who think as I do. It is important, however, that we understand clearly that these concepts are just ways of seeing. The recent Iranian edict that couples may not kiss with sexual feeling is an example of how a concept, in this case sexual purity, can inhibit the human spirit.

Society, the Buddha Sangha included, is simply a bundle of shared views — which are essentially empty. Our task is to be free from blind attachment to particular views and to see clearly into that which has no form at all.

1983

The head and tail are the two aspects of Zen practice, realization and application. It is important to understand how these two archetypal terms can be transmuted into our daily lives.

Realization is experience of how things are and how we ourselves are. It is necessarily incomplete. "Even Shākyamuni is only halfway there," and so we too have our limitations. Our realization is our own best wisdom at any one time.

Application is the compassion that arises with our wisdom. It too is imperfect, but it is our own personal best, always under reevaluation and correction. It is our teaching, not an overt expression of morality, but a style that is formed from inside. When we act, we can ask ourselves, "Is this my way of teaching?"

1985

All Zen Buddhist temples in the Far East have a "mountain name" as well as a temple name. For example, Ryūtakuji (Dragon-Marsh Temple) is also known as Entsūsan (Complete Passage Mountain). Even city temples have mountain names.

The temple name sometimes resonates with the surroundings. For example, Dragon-Marsh Temple is located near the village of Sawaji (Marshy Place). The mountain name usually expresses an ideal of the practice, for example, passing through all delusions.

We in Western Zen Buddhism have not generally adopted this custom in naming our temples. It is instructive nonetheless. Also instructive is the way old teachers got their own names. The early Japanese teacher Kanzan's name means "Mountain of Kan" ("Mountain of Barrier"). "Kan" or "Barrier" had been his kōan, the way we use Mu.

Take your own name accordingly. Become Mu Mountain on your cushions.

1985

The Zen path is the path of the Tathāgata; that is to say, it is the Buddha arising as Buddha Nature. Realization of this Buddha does not occur out there someplace, but with the very person reading these words. Words can be skillful means that bring us back to this person, back home to silence and peace — to find comfort in the song of the thrush and in the smiles of our friends.

Shikantaza (pure sitting) is the basic form of zazen. In this practice, you bring yourself to a complete stop with each breath-moment. There is no sequence. When you quietly inhale, everything stops. When you quietly exhale, everything stops. A thought may appear, but there is nothing before it and nothing follows it. You may hear something or otherwise sense something, but it too comes from nowhere, and you do not pursue it with thinking. The practice of breath-counting can help you to learn shikantaza, focusing just on each single point in the sequence. Kōan practice is established on shikantaza. Learn shikantaza and you learn zazen.

Is there something equivalent to Zen Buddhist understanding in other religious practices? When this question was asked in class the other evening, I wanted to say "No" and "Yes" at the same time. "Yes" is the general answer and "No" is the specific. Generally, there is indeed perennial wisdom. Specifically, each religious mode is its own being. Is there a position from which one can judge them all? I don't know, really.

1987

Spoofs are an important part of any religious tradition for they add new perspectives. When they are excluded as sacrilegious the tradition suffers. This is especially true when the spoof is in touch with the mystery in its own way. Thus *Monkey*, the great spoof of Chinese tradition, is a fine teacher.[80]

In presenting their new perspectives, however, spoofs are by their nature hard on the old ones. Kabir, for example:

> *Qazi, what book are you lecturing on?*
> *Yak yak yak, day and night.*
> *You never had an original thought.*
> *Feeling your power, you circumcise —*
> *I can't go along with that, brother.*
> *If your God favored circumcision,*
> *Why didn't you come out cut?*[81]

"Blasphemy!" cry the Mullahs, as they did in response to Salman Rushdie's *Satanic Verses*.

1989

As I write this, our teacher, Yamada Kōun Rōshi lies dying at his home in Kamakura. He appears in my dreams, healthy and hearty, and I feel his presence as I recite sutras with the Sangha here and as I work at my desk.

Anne Aitken and I met Rōshi when he was the senior student

of Yasutani Rōshi at the Kamakura Zazenkai in the fall of 1961, almost twenty-eight years ago. Since then he has been so much a part of our lives, we can hardly imagine that he will soon be gone.

In 1969, Yasutani Rōshi led his last sesshin in Hawaii, and we sought again to persuade our former teacher, Nakagawa Sōen Rōshi, to resume his visits to the United States to lead sesshins. He did come a couple of times, but it became clear that he could not continue. By then Yamada Rōshi was established as a teacher, so we asked him to guide us. He accepted the invitation and came twice in the first year, and once a year thereafter until 1985.

He saved my life, for Zen was my life and my path was like Zen Lane in downtown Honolulu: all signs said "Dead End."[82] He saved our Sangha and its members too, for we had no leadership and were floundering.

Now the Diamond Sangha is a lively organism, serving the Honolulu community and offering a practice place for people on the Mainland, in Australia, in Latin America, and in Europe. None of this would be possible without Yamada Rōshi's generous gift of his wisdom and compassion. I vow to make my life a repayment of his kindness and to carry on as a successor worthy of his genius. Like all vows, this one can never be fulfilled, but it will be a light on my path.

1990

Late last year, Joseph Cardinal Ratzinger, a prefect of the Catholic Church, issued a "Letter to the Bishops of the Catholic Church on Some Aspects of Christian Meditation." This was an attempt to correct meditation practices among Catholics, including those he termed "Eastern methods," by which, he explained in a footnote, he referred to "methods which are inspired by Hinduism and Buddhism, such as 'Zen,' 'Transcendental Meditation,' or 'Yoga.'"

Some of my friends and colleagues are exercised by this document, and while I question many of its points, still I find some points could be instructive for us when they are taken from their Christian context — for example, the message quoted from St. Augustine: "Don't remain within yourself." Ha! That's right! Don't close yourself off!

Another example would be the writer's caution against assuming that certain superficial experiences, such as feelings of warmth and relaxation, or perceptions of light, can be anything ultimately significant. That's right too! Who is seeing that bright light?

Ta-hui Tsung-kao was a Lin-chi master who lived in the first half of the twelfth century. He was a Dharma successor of Yüan-wu, editor of the *Blue Cliff Record*, and is best known for his firm support of kōan study. His letters and talks were translated by Christopher Cleary in his *Swampland Flowers*. Here's one of his stories:

> *In the old days, Kuei-shan asked Lazy An, "What work do you do during the twenty-four hours of the day?"*
> *Lazy An said, "I tend an ox."*
> *Kuei-shan said, "How do you tend it?"*
> *Lazy An said, "Whenever it gets into the grass, I pull it back by the nose."*
> *Kuei-shan said, "You're really tending the ox."*[83]

"Grass" is shorthand for delusive thoughts, which includes all thoughts when practicing zazen, and extraneous thoughts when occupied with a task. Kuei-shan and Ta-hui appeal to each of us to practice watchfully, during each of the twenty-four hours, each of the sixty minutes, each of the sixty seconds.

There are two points here. First a broad spectrum of past teachers can be our inspiration, from Pai-chang, credited with creating the Zen Buddhist monastic rules, to P'u-hua, who wandered the streets like a free spirit, ringing his little bell and talking to himself.

The second point relates to gratitude and the things that go with gratitude: loyalty and responsibility. We may be restating the Dharma in Western terms in our Zen centers, but the old teachers keep us on track.

Recently someone asked me, "What do you get out of your practice these days?" I was a little taken aback. I don't usually think about practice in terms of results and I don't usually think much about myself. Yet there is no reason why I should not.

The first meaning of practice for me is zazen. What does zazen give me? Liberation from tension and worry, I would say. It keeps me sane. It gives me rest where there is no coming or going. It also gives me inspiration from time to time. Good ideas pop into my head from nowhere and these too are liberating, not from tension and worry, but from limitations I didn't know I had.

In my practice apart from zazen, my psychic income is more varied. It includes a delight in Sangha relations and again it also includes the liberation that comes from good ideas, and from their formulation. I feel blessed by these ideas, appearing in words from my students and in my own words. In preparing a glossary recently, I came to "Rebirth." This is the way I crafted the entry:

> *Rebirth.* The coherent, changing karma of an individual or a cluster of individuals reappearing after death. The continuous arising of coherent, changing karma during life. Distinguish from Reincarnation.

A mini-teishō, inspiring to realize, fun to put together, and maybe even instructive for others. And that's my coherent, changing karma.

In her essay, "Reflections on the Right Use of School Studies," Simone Weil cites an Eskimo story about the origin of light: "In the eternal darkness, the crow, unable to find any food, longed for light, and the earth was illuminated." She goes on to say, "If there is a real desire, if the thing desired is really light, then the desire for light produces it. There is a real desire when there is an effort of attention." [84]

In Buddhist terms it is Bodhichitta, the desire for enlightenment, that fuels our patient attention. There is more. Weil goes on to suggest that while desire is one aspect of attention, the acknowledgment of one's own mediocrity is the other.

This acknowledgment, which Weil describes as a sense of one's stupidity, can be rendered in our context as openness. If you establish a set of values and standards for the practice then you obscure the light, no matter how cogent your values and standards may be. But with humility, poverty of spirit, you are open to the light in its full brilliance.

Dōgen Zenji urges us to "muster body and mind" and this is the power of Bodhichitta. He also cites the poet Su Tung-po, who was enlightened by the sound of the brook in the middle of the night. [85] Su Tung-po was receptive to the sound of the water, as Te-shan was receptive to the sudden darkness when Lung-t'an blew out the candle, as the Head Monk Ming was receptive to Hui-neng's question about his original nature. [86]

Sometimes people express doubts about their faith and I would anticipate hearing similar doubts about attention. But just as you would be fully enlightened with total faith, so every event would confirm your being if you mustered fully receptive attention. Nobody's perfect and we're all on the path.

Death and the Afterlife

1981

Years ago, I asked Yamada Rōshi about life after death. He replied, "Of course there is always the phenomenal side." He was referring to the numerator of the universe which endlessly unfolds. His answer has remained with me, enriching my insight into fundamental questions of soul and no-soul. The Buddha challenged the idea of an immutable soul. He said nothing about the mutable soul, and its survival, though his successors in most streams of Buddhism have had a lot to say on this subject. For all their words, the question of what happens when one dies remains a mystery.

1990

Consider a healthy plant that is growing from its top. It will have buds lower down on the stem but they will just sit there without developing. If you nip off the top of the plant, however, then the buds on the stem will suddenly sprout and you will soon have a plant with many branches. The whole world is a plant like this. Living beings are the growing tip of Essential Nature, and if you cut this tip, then the force that brought forth oxygen, lichen, grasses, and all the trees, animals, birds, and fishes of the world will break out somewhere else in the world, or somewhere else in the universe, perhaps in very different forms.

If human beings die out, then the buds of language and speculation among primates and cetaceans will surely burst forth, or if they don't survive either, among some other beings after a time. I am sure of this. It's not mere hope but is the way things are in this vast Milky Way and beyond.

It's hard to accept the possibility of humanity dying, with our many kinds of learning and art and music, with the hopes of countless mothers and fathers who brought forth children with trust in the future. It's even harder to accept the possibility of the Earth itself dying, with its millions of years of gradual evolution through countless species of plants and insects and animals and birds in rich diversity. It is our responsibility to devote ourselves to save the Earth and its beings, and this we vow to do every day: "The many beings are numberless, I vow to save them." And in the work of fulfilling our vows, we are supporting the incredible creativity of empty universal nature — ready to burst forth with living beings wherever there is a chance for them. It is this incredible potency that gives hope to our work.

NOTES

1.   Syllabus, The Zen Buddhist Sutra Book: "The Great Prajñā Pāramitā Heart Sūtra."

2.   Cf. Yūhō Yokoi, *Zen Master Dōgen: An Introduction with Selected Writings* (New York: Weatherhill, 1976), p. 28. Eisai was echoing Nan-ch'üan, see Thomas Cleary, trans., *Book of Serenity* (Hudson, N.Y.: Lindisfarne Press, 1990), p. 290.

3.   Fr. Willigis Jäger, "Zen and Religion," *Blind Donkey*, vol. 9, no. 4 (January 1987), pp. 13–25.

4.   Wu-men Hui-k'ai. Syllabus, *Wu-men kuan*, Case I.

5.   Cf. William F. Powell, *The Record of Tung-shan* (Honolulu: University of Hawaii Press, 1986), p. 62.

6.   Raymond B. Blakney, *Meister Eckhart: A Modern Translation* (New York & London: Harper & Bros., 1941), p. 17.

7.   Translated from the Chinese in Yaichiro Isobe, *Musings of a Chinese Vegetarian* (Tokyo: Yuhodo, 1926), p. 69. See also William Scott Wilson, trans., *Roots of Wisdom: Saikontan, by Hung Ying-ming* (New York: Kodansha International, 1985), p. 51.

8. Walpola Rahula, *What the Buddha Taught* (New York: Grove Press, 1959), pp. 53–54.

9. Isobe, *Musings of a Chinese Vegetarian*, p. 4. See also Wilson, *Roots of Wisdom*, p. 24.

10. Robert Aitken, *The Gateless Barrier: The Wu-men kuan (Mumonkan)*, translated and with a commentary (San Francisco: North Point Press, 1990), p. 126.

11. Benjamin Lee Whorf, "An American Indian Model of the Universe," *Teachings from the American Earth*, Dennis Tedlock and Barbara Tedlock, eds. (New York: Liveright, 1975), p. 126.

12. Aitken, *The Gateless Barrier*, p. 126.

13. Thomas Cleary and J. C. Cleary, *The Blue Cliff Record* (Boston: Shambhala, 1992), p. 297.

14. The Buddha Shākyamuni's words upon his realization, according to the *Denkōroku*. Cf. Thomas Cleary, trans., *Transmission of Light* (San Francisco: North Point Press, 1990), p. 3.

15. Dōgen Kigen, "Kyōjukaimon." See Syllabus, The Zen Buddhist Sutra Book: The Jukai Ceremony, "The Three Pure Precepts." Also, Robert Aitken, *The Mind of Clover: Essays in Zen Buddhist Ethics* (San Francisco: North Point Press, 1984), pp. 15, 180–81.

16. Translated and quoted by R. H. Blyth, *Zen in English Literature and Oriental Classics* (New York: Dutton, 1960), pp. 20–21.

17. Frederick Franck, *Art as a Way: A Return to the Spiritual Roots* (New York: Crossroads, 1982), p. 24.

18. Franz Boenders, "Introduction," in *Frederick Franck, Recent Paintings and Drawings* (Leiden: Galerie Amber, 1991), p. 2.

19. Franck, *Art as a Way*, epigraph.

20. Kazuaki Tanahashi et al., trans., *Moon in a Dewdrop: Writings of Zen Master Dōgen* (San Francisco: North Point Press, 1985), p. 46.

21. See Syllabus, Glossary. Also, Richard A. Gard, ed., *Buddhism* (New York: George Braziller, 1962), pp. 146–47.

22.   The crisis hinged on alleged exploitations by Shimano Eidō Rōshi of his women students.

23.   Cf. Ruth Fuller Sasaki et al., trans., *The Recorded Sayings of Layman P'ang: A Ninth Century Zen Classic* (New York: Weatherhill, 1971), p. 46.

24.   See D. T. Suzuki, *Manual of Zen Buddhism* (New York: Grove Press, 1960).

25.   See Syllabus, The Zen Buddhist Sutra Book: "Purification."

26.   See Syllabus, Jukai Ceremony: "The Ten Grave Precepts." Also, Aitken, *The Mind of Clover*, pp. 3–104.

27.   Thomas Cleary, trans., *The Flower Ornament Scripture: A Translation of the Avatamsaka Sutra*, 3 vols. (Boston: Shambhala, 1984–1987), I:212–29; III:340, 347.

28.   Cleary and Cleary, *The Blue Cliff Record*, p. 558.

29.   Virginia Woolf, *Jacob's Room* and *The Waves* (New York: Harcourt, Brace and World, 1959), p. 90.

30.   This is the closing mantra of the Heart Sutra. Syllabus, The Zen Buddhist Sutra Book: "The Great Prajñā Pāramitā Heart Sutra."

31.   *Sangha*, a special issue of *Hoto*, Los Altos, Calif., Spring, 1981.

32.   Elizabeth Bisland, ed., *The Japanese Letters of Lafcadio Hearn* (Boston: Houghton Mifflin, 1911), p. 40.

33.   John Blofeld, trans., *The Zen Teaching of Huang Po: On the Transmission of Mind* (New York: Grove Press, 1958), p. 36.

34.   Cleary and Cleary, *The Blue Cliff Record*, p. 554.

35.   Ibid., p. 37.

36.   Charlotte Joko Beck, *Everyday Zen* (San Francisco: Harper & Row, 1989), pp. 49–52.

37.   Cleary and Cleary, *The Blue Cliff Record*, p. 1.

38.   Aitken, *The Gateless Barrier*, p. 126.

39.   Cf. Thomas Cleary, trans., *Book of Serenity*, p. 86.

40.   Haku'un Yasutani, "Introductory Lectures on Zen Training,"

Philip Kapleau, *The Three Pillars of Zen: Teaching, Practice, and Enlightenment* (Boston: Beacon Press, 1965), p. 28.

41.   J. Baird Callicott and Roger T. Ames, *Nature in Asian Traditions of Thought: Essays in Environmental Philosophy* (Albany, N.Y.: State University of New York Press, 1989), pp. 25–36.

42.   Paul Shepard, *Thinking Animals: Animals and the Development of Human Intelligence* (New York: Viking Press, 1978).

43.   Philip B. Yampolsky, *The Platform Sutra of the Sixth Patriarch* (New York: Columbia University Press, 1967), pp. 1–110.

44.   Isshū Miura and Ruth Fuller Sasaki, *Zen Dust: The History of the Koan and Koan Study in Rinzai (Lin-chi) Zen* (New York: Harcourt, Brace and World, 1966), pp. 151–52, 229–30.

45.   Aitken, *The Gateless Barrier*, pp. 19–21, 163; Cleary and Cleary, *The Blue Cliff Record*, p. 216.

46.   Aitken, *The Gateless Barrier*, p. 160.

47.   Ibid., p. 7.

48.   Cf. Tanahashi, *Moon in a Dewdrop*, p. 200.

49.   A. F. Price, *The Diamond Sutra* in *The Diamond Sutra and The Sutra of Hui Neng* (Berkeley: Shambhala, 1969), pp. 41–42.

50.   Hee Jin Kim, *Dōgen Kigen: Mytstical Realist* (Tucson: University of Arizona Press, 1987), p. 84.

51.   Aitken, *The Gateless Barrier*, p. 100.

52.   Kim, *Dōgen Kigen*, p. 189.

53.   Cf. A. L. Sadler, *The Ten Foot Square Hut* and *Tales of the Heike* (Sydney: Angus and Robertson, 1928), p. 1.

54.   Cleary, *The Blue Cliff Record*, p. 72.

55.   An echo of a sutra dedication, translated by Nakagawa Sōen Rōshi. See Syllabus, The Zen Buddhist Sutra Book: "First Sutra Service Dedication":

> *Let true Dharma continue,*
> *Sangha relations become complete.*

56. Syllabus, The Zen Buddhist Sutra Book, "Hakuin Zenji: 'Song of Zazen.'"

57. Giei Sato and Eshin Nishimura, *Unsui: A Diary of Zen Monastic Life* (Honolulu: University of Hawaii, 1973), Plate 59.

58. R. H. Mathews, *Chinese-English Dictionary* (Cambridge, Mass.: Harvard University Press, 1969), entry 1123.

59. Syllabus, The Zen Buddhist Sutra Book: "The Great Prajñā Pāramitā Heart Sutra."

60. See Syllabus, Zen Buddhist Sutra Book: "Hakuin Zenji: 'Song of Zazen.'"

61. "Musō Kokushi's Admonitions" in Suzuki, *Manual of Zen Buddhism*, p. 150.

62. Hee Jin Kim, "'The Reason of Words and Letters': Dōgen and Kōan Language," in William R. LaFleur, ed., *Dōgen Studies* (Honolulu: University of Hawaii, 1985), pp. 54–82.

63. Ibid., pp. 57–58.

64. Seikan Hasegawa, *The Cave of Poison Grass: Notes on the Hannya Sutra* (Arlington, Va.: Great Ocean Publishers, 1985), p. 169.

65. Cf. Tanahashi, *Moon in a Dewdrop*, p. 70.

66. Trevor Leggett, *Zen and the Ways* (Boulder, Colo.: Shambhala, 1978), especially pp. 55–57.

67. "Introductory Kōans," Mimeo. Diamond Sangha, Honolulu.

68. Nechung Rinpoché, "Everything That Comes Together Disperses," *Dra-Yang* (Pahala, Hawaii: n.d.).

69. Philip Sherrard, *The Eclipse of Man and Nature: An Inquiry into the Origins and Consequences of Modern Science* (West Stockbridge, Mass.: Lindisfarne Press, 1987), pp. 41–42.

70. Thomas Cleary, *Entry into the Inconceivable: An Introduction to Huayen Buddhism* (Honolulu: University of Hawaii Press, 1983), p. 37.

71. Cleary, *Transmission of Light*, p. 3.

72. Syllabus, Zen Buddhist Sutra Book: Mealtime Sutras, "The Spirit of Acceptance."

73. Italo Calvino, *Six Memos for the Next Millennium* (Cambridge, Mass.: Harvard University Press, 1988), pp. 21–22.

74. Callicott and Ames, *Nature in Asian Traditions of Thought*, pp. 67–78.

75. Organized resistance to the storage of nuclear weapons at Waikele Gulch in central Oahu led to their removal to West Loch within the confines of Pearl Harbor, where resisters are barred.

76. William Jordan, *Divorce among the Gulls: An Uncommon Look at Human Nature* (San Francisco: North Point Press, 1991).

77. Roger Callen, geologist and paleontologist in Adelaide, South Australia, a Diamond Sangha member, writes in comment to this generalization: "Jordan is wrong in saying the smallest increment the fossil record can resolve is 100,000 years. Using spores and pollen, one can resolve increments of 10,000 years in the Tertiary. With various forms of isotope and TL dating one can resolve hundreds of years in the Quaternary. In general, resolution improves with youngness of rocks. Also, with isotope dating in the remote past, it is now even possible to resolve intervals of a few thousand years."

A salutary reminder to keep the metaphor accurate! The point of the metaphor, however inaccurate, remains. The span of human civilization has indeed been like a flash, and questions of survival, human and nonhuman, remain.

78. Callen comments further, "You are correct in saying the impact of an asteroid will be indistinguishable from the destruction created by man, in terms of species eliminated, but the two can be distinguished by other methods. One can say whether it was an asteroid or some predator which produced the effect."

79. Aitken, *The Gateless Barrier*, p. 121.

80. Arthur Waley, trans., *Monkey* (New York: John Day, 1943).

81. Linda Hess and Shukdev Singh, *The Bījak of Kabir* (San Francisco: North Point Press, 1983), p. 69.

82. Named after a prominent Asian-American family named Zen.

83.   Christopher Cleary, *Swampland Flowers: Letters and Lectures of Zen Master Ta Hui* (New York: Grove Press, 1977), p. 3.

84.   Simone Weil, *Waiting for God* (New York: Harper and Row, 1973), p. 107.

85.   Kim, *Dōgen Kigen*, pp. 100, 188–89.

86.   Aitken, *The Gateless Barrier*, pp. 147, 177.

The Syllabus

INTRODUCTION

In the course of ardent practice, a student will sometimes experience the sacred in a most personal way with *makyō*, the "uncanny realm." During zazen, kinhin, a sutra service, or even in free time during or soon after a sesshin, suddenly one is playing a pivotal role in an ancient ritual. Perhaps this very body is indeed the Buddha, covered with gold leaf. Makyō are often dismissed by teachers as mere dreams, but they can be profoundly encouraging, for when they have passed, the ongoing practice is intimately personal and meaningful.*

Words and procedures of a Zen Buddhist ritual evoke the sacred realm that appears spontaneously in makyō. Our rites are a reenactment of those of the Buddha with his disciples. They are

---

* The term *makyō* can also refer to "Alice in Wonderland" experiences of bodily distortion, which are on the fringe of deeper possibilities. See Aitken, *The Gateless Barrier*, pp. 161–63.

the Buddha and his disciples conducting them in our dōjō with our own bodies.

Like makyō, ritual is a drama. In the Zen Buddhist hall, it includes chanting, bowing, and circumambulation with bells and drums in relation to a central altar. The zazen itself is ritual. These elements, with the precise arrangement of cushions and the orientation to the four directions, are arcana, primordial presentations of the sacred in a meaningful and dynamic cluster. In their repetition they are empowered more and more.

In this evocation of the sacred into the secular, all beings are sanctified, purified, enlightened — celebrating the authority of the timeless. Still, time passes, conditions change, and as Western Buddhists we are faced with the need to evoke in another language, to add whole segments, and to drop others. We must be as careful as we can in this process.

Risky business, but all Western centers have dared to try it, to a greater or lesser degree. But the basics remain among all that are worthy of being called Zen Buddhist. This Syllabus includes an outline of the words and procedures used in Zen Buddhist practice in the Diamond Sangha tradition.

By way of orientation, I begin the Syllabus with a Lattice of the Dharma, listing the various elements of the teaching as a minimal kind of metaphysical framework. There you will find the Four Noble Truths, the Eightfold Path, the Three Bodies of the Buddha, the Three Treasures, and other classical outlines of the truth which the Buddha experienced. They are in a bare form, and can be clothed by references to the Glossary, in many cases to the Zen Buddhist Sutra Book, by further study in other texts, and by your own attention to their implications. For those interested in kōan practice, I have added Case I of the *Wu-men kuan,* with Wu-men's commentary and poem. It is the basis of the kōan Mu, to which many of the "Words in the Dōjō" are directed.

The Zen Buddhist Sutra Book comes next. It is a very small, simple collection in comparison to some. We keep some sutras in the Sino-Japanese and even in the Pali, others we recite in a translated form. Some we do both ways. We leave out certain dhāranīs, hymns of praise whose literal meaning has been lost, and we add several sutra dedications.

The dedications are called *ekō* in Sino-Japanese, literally "turning." They are the turning of any merit acquired by reciting the sutras back to our ancestral teachers, and back to the process of all beings enlightening themselves. The sutras are our gifts to the world, chanted in gratitude for the way of wisdom and compassion that is affirmed more deeply with each service.

The Sutra Book is headed by a Sequence of Services. Like other Western Zen Buddhist centers, we hold brief services each morning and evening on ordinary days, and longer ones during sesshins. Formal meals have an extensive ritual, informal meals just a brief gāthā. I have included a ceremony of Jukai, the ritual of affirming oneself as a disciple of the Buddha and a follower of his Precepts and have added a few words of explanation before most of the sections.

Following the Sutra Book is a segment on sesshin that includes a schedule, an outline of leadership responsibility, and Yasutani Haku'un Rōshi's "Three Essentials of Sesshin." Then there is a description of the percussion instruments used in a medium-size Zen Buddhist center, ranging from the tiny bell used for wakeup, to drums of various timbres, to the big bell that booms over the neighborhood.

Next is an extensive glossary of Zen Buddhist terms and usages, including many English words that have taken Buddhist significance. "Evil," for example, is not connected to Original Sin, which, incidentally, you will not find listed. The Glossary is another kind of Lattice of the Dharma that can form the basis for further study. Finally, I offer a Bibliography, with suggestions about where one might focus in each book.

Many Zen Buddhist teachers advise their students not to read. I can't agree with this. Words convey the Dharma, and in well-translated books with cogent commentaries one can find true teishōs. Zazen remains central to the practice, and every virtue of the Dharma arises from there, as Hakuin Zenji says. But even the Buddha did not remain seated under the Bodhi tree and he taught even himself with his inspired words. As Buddhists, it is our responsibility to poke around in good libraries and bookstores.

"Dharma gates are countless, I vow to wake to them."*

---

* The Zen Buddhist Sutra Book: "Great Vows for All."

LATTICE OF THE DHARMA

See also the Zen Buddhist Sutra Book and the Glossary.

The Four Noble Truths:

1. Anguish is everywhere.
2. There is a cause of anguish.
3. There is liberation from anguish.
4. Liberation is the Eightfold Path.

The Eightfold Path:

1. Right Views
2. Right Thoughts
3. Right Speech
4. Right Conduct
5. Right Livelihood

6. Right Effort *or* Life-style

7. Right Recollection

8. Right Absorption

The Three Bodies of the Buddha:

1. The pure empty body

2. The bliss body of mutual interdependence

3. The transformation body of uniqueness

The Four Abodes:

1. Loving-kindness

2. Compassion

3. Joy in the liberation of others

4. Equanimity *or* Impartiality

The Pāramitās, or Perfections

The Six Pāramitās:

1. Dāna (Giving)

2. Shīla (Morality)

3. Kshānti (Forbearance)

4. Vīrya (Vitality or Zeal)

5. Dhyāna (Focused Meditation)

6. Prajñā (Wisdom)

The Four Additional Pāramitās:

7. Upāya (Skillful Means)

8. Pranidhāna (Resolve)

9. Bala (Strength)

10. Jñāna (Knowledge)

The Three Poisons:

1. Greed

2. Hatred

3. Ignorance

The Sixteen Bodhisattva Precepts

Refuge in the Three Treasures:

1. I take refuge in the Buddha.

2. I take refuge in the Dharma.

3. I take refuge in the Sangha.

The Three Pure Precepts:

1. To maintain the Precepts

2. To practice all good dharmas

3. To save the many beings

The Ten Grave Precepts:

1. Not to kill

2. Not to steal

3. Not to misuse sex

4. Not to speak falsely

5. Not to give or take drugs

6. Not to discuss faults of others

7. Not to praise myself while abusing others

8. Not to spare the Dharma assets

9. Not to indulge in anger

10. Not to defame the Three Treasures

The Six Realms:

1. Devils
2. Hungry Ghosts
3. Animals
4. Titans
5. Humans
6. Devas

The Eighteen Dhātus:

Organ	*Field*	*Consciousness*
1. Eye	Form and Color	Seeing
2. Ear	Sound	Hearing
3. Nose	Scent	Smelling
4. Tongue	Flavor	Tasting
5. Body	The Tangible	Feeling
6. Mind	Thought	Thinking

The Five Skandhas:

1. Forms of the world
2. Sensation
3. Perception
4. Formulation
5. Consciousness

The Four Bodhisattva Vows:

1. To save the many beings
2. To abandon greed, hatred, and ignorance
3. To wake to the countless teachings
4. To embody the Way of the Buddha

WU-MEN KUAN: CASE I*

The Case:

> A monk asked Chao-chou, "Has the dog Buddha-nature
> or not?"
>   Chao-chou said, "Mu."

Wu-men's Comment:

For the practice of Zen, it is imperative that you pass through the
barrier set up by the Ancestral Teachers. For subtle realization, it
is of the utmost importance that you cut off the mind road. If
you do not pass the barrier of the ancestors, if you do not cut off
the mind road, then you are a ghost clinging to bushes and grasses.

What is the barrier of the Ancestral Teachers? It is just this
one word "Mu" — the one barrier of our faith. We call it the

---

* Robert Aitken, *The Gateless Barrier: The Wu-men kuan (Mumonkan)* (San Francisco:
North Point Press, 1990), pp. 7–9.

Gateless Barrier of the Zen tradition. When you pass through this barrier, you will not only interview Chao-chou intimately. You will walk hand in hand with all the Ancestral Teachers in the successive generations of our lineage — the hair of your eyebrows entangled with theirs, seeing with the same eyes, hearing with the same ears. Won't that be fulfilling? Is there anyone who would not want to pass this barrier?

So, then, make your whole body a mass of doubt, and with your three hundred and sixty bones and joints and your eighty-four thousand hair follicles concentrate on this one word "Mu." Day and night, keep digging into it. Don't consider it to be nothingness. Don't think in terms of "has" and "has not." It is like swallowing a red-hot iron ball. You try to vomit it out, but you cannot.

Gradually you purify yourself, eliminating mistaken knowledge and attitudes you have held from the past. Inside and outside become one. You're like a mute person who has had a dream — you know it for yourself alone.

Suddenly Mu breaks open. The heavens are astonished, the earth is shaken. It is as though you have snatched the great sword of General Kuan. When you meet the Buddha, you kill the Buddha. When you meet Bodhidharma, you kill Bodhidharma. At the very cliff edge of birth-and-death, you find the Great Freedom. In the Six Worlds and the Four Modes of Birth, you enjoy a Samādhi of frolic and play.

How, then, should you work with it? Exhaust all your life energy on this one word "Mu." If you do not falter, then it's done! A single spark lights your Dharma candle.

Wu-men's Verse:

> *Dog, Buddha nature —*
> *the full presentation of the whole;*
> *with a bit of "has" or "has not"*
> *body is lost, life is lost.*

THE ZEN BUDDHIST
SUTRA BOOK

Schedule of Services

Each service begins and ends with three raihai, or prostrations. Formal meal services are held during sesshin. Both formal and informal meal services are held on days other than sesshin.

Sesshin

Morning

"Purification"
"Vandana"
"Ti-Sarana"
"The Great Prajñā Pāramitā Heart Sutra" or "Maka Hannya Haramita Shin Gyō"
"Shō Sai Myō Kichijō Darani"
First Sutra Service Dedication

"Tōrei Zenji: 'Bodhisattva's Vow' "
"Enmei Jikku Kannon Gyō"
Second Sutra Service Dedication
"Great Vows for All"

Before Teishō
  "On Opening the Dharma"

After Teishō
  "Great Vows for All" (in Sino-Japanese)

Evening
  "Hakuin Zenji: 'Song of Zazen' "
  Sesshin Evening Service Dedication
  "Great Vows for All"
  Evening Message

At the End of Sesshin
  "Maka Hannya Haramita Shin Gyō"
  Sesshin Ending Dedication or Jukai Ceremony
  "Great Vows for All"

Daily

  Morning
    "The Great Prajñā Pāramitā Heart Sutra" or "Maka
      Hannya Haramita Shin Gyō"
    "Sho Sai Myō Kichijō Darani"
    Early Morning Service Dedication

  Before Evening Zazen
    "Purification"
    "Enmei Jikku Kannon Gyō"
    Daily Evening Service Dedication

After Evening Zazen
"Great Vows for All"

The Gāthās[1]

The gāthā is a verse that sums up a particular aspect of the Dharma, often expressing a vow. It is probably the earliest form in the Buddhist liturgy.

Purification

A gāthā-vow from the *Hua-yen Sutra* that has become the prologue to most Zen Buddhist services.[2] It is recited at evening services daily and at the morning services during sesshin.

> All the evil karma, ever created by me since of old,
> on account of my beginningless greed, hatred and
>   ignorance,
> born of my conduct, speech and thought,
> I now confess openly and fully.

---

[1] Give Latin value to vowels in Pali or Sino-Japanese, except as indicated. Hold the doubled consonant in Sino-Japanese twice as long as the single one.

[2] Thomas Cleary, *The Flower Ornament Scripture*, 3 vols. (Boston: Shambhala, 1987), III:383.

Vandana

The traditional gāthā of veneration to the Buddha, recited in the original Pali language at morning services during sesshin.

> *Namo tassa bhagavato arahato sammasambuddhassa.*
> I venerate the Sacred One, the Great Sage, the
> Truly Enlightened One.

Ti-Sarana

The traditional Threefold Vow of Refuge recited in the Pali, affirming a home in Buddha, Dharma, Sangha. It is the initiation and reinitiation to the Way of the Buddha found in all Buddhist centers. It is recited at morning services during sesshin. Pronounce "gacchāmi" as "guhchāmi."

> *Buddham saranam gacchāmi;*
> I take refuge in the Buddha;
> *dhammam saranam gacchāmi;*
> I take refuge in the Dharma;
> *sangham saranam gacchāmi.*
> I take refuge in the Sangha.

On Opening the Dharma

Traditional gāthā recited before the teishō at all Zen centers.

> *The Dharma, incomparably profound and minutely
> subtle,*

is rarely encountered, even in hundreds of thousands of
  millions of kalpas;
we now can see it, listen to it, accept and hold it;
may we completely realize the Tathāgata's true meaning.

Great Vows for All

These are the "Four Bodhisattva Vows," recited in most Mahayana centers at the close of ceremonies.

Shu jō mu hen sei gan do
The many beings are numberless, I vow to save
  them,
bonnō mu jin sei gan dan
greed, hatred, and ignorance rise endlessly, I vow
  to abandon them,
ho mon mu ryō sei gan gaku
Dharma-gates are countless, I vow to wake to
  them,
butsu dō mu jō sei gan jō.
Buddha's Way is unsurpassed, I vow to embody
  it fully.

The Sutras and a Dhāranī

Sutras, literally the "warp" of the Dharma, are sermons of the
Buddha, those attributed to him, and by limited extension, those
of his successors. The dhāranī (Japanese: Darani) is a hymn of
praise, transliterated from the Sanskrit through the Chinese and
then the Japanese, Korean, or Vietnamese.

Maka Hannya Haramita Shin Gyō
The Great Prajñā Pāramitā Heart Sutrā

The classical condensation of the six-hundred-volume Prajñā Pāra-mitā literature, translated into Chinese by Hsüan-tang in the seventh century, can be called the basic Mahayana sutra. Known as the "Heart Sutra," it is recited in early morning services on ordinary days, and during the morning services at sesshin. The acute accent on the letter *e* in the next to the last line is inserted as an aid to pronunciation.

Kan ji zai bo sa gyō jin han-nya ha ra mi ta ji
Avalokiteshvara Bodhisattva, practicing deep
　　Prajñā Pāramitā,
shō ken go on kai kū do is-sai ku yaku.
clearly saw that all five skandhas[3] are empty,
　　transforming anguish and distress.
Sha ri shi shiki fu i ku ku fu i shiki
Shāriputra, form is no other than emptiness,
　　emptiness no other than form;
shiki soku ze ku ku soku ze shiki
form is exactly emptiness, emptiness exactly
　　form;
jū sō gyō shiki yaku bu nyo ze
sensation, perception, formulation,
　　consciousness are also like this.
Sha ri shi ze shō hō kū sō fu shō fu metsu
Shāriputra, all things are essentially empty — not
　　born, not destroyed;

---

[3] The five "bundles" that make up the self: forms of the world, sensation, perception, mental reaction, and consciousness.

fu ku fu jō fu zō fu gen

not stained, not pure; without loss, without gain.

ze ko kū chū mu shiki mu ju sō gyō shiki

Therefore in emptiness there is no form, no
 sensation, perception, formulation,
 consciousness;

mu gen-ni bi zes-shin i

no eye, ear, nose, tongue, body, mind,

mu shiki shō kō mi soku hō

no color, sound, scent, taste, touch, thought;

mu gen kai nai shi mu i shiki kai

no seeing and so on to no thinking;[4]

mu mu myō yaku mu mu myō jin

no ignorance and also no ending of ignorance,

nai shi mu rō shi yaku mu rō shi jin

and so on to no old age and death and also no
 ending of old age and death;[5]

mu ku shu metsu dō

no anguish, cause of anguish, cessation, path;[6]

mu chi yaku mu toku i mu shō tok'ko

no wisdom and no attainment. Since there is
 nothing to attain,

bo dai sat-ta e han-nya ha ra mi ta

the Bodhisattva lives by Prajñā Pāramitā,

ko shim-mu kei ge mu kei ge ko mu u ku fu

with no hindrance in the mind; no hindrance and
 therefore no fear;

on ri is-sai ten dō mu sō ku gyō ne han

---

[4] The six senses, the six qualities that are sensed, and the six kinds of consciousness
form the Eighteen Dhatus, or Categories.

[5] Refers to the Twelve-linked Chain of Causation.

[6] The Four Noble Truths: Anguish is everywhere, there is a cause of anguish, there
is liberation from anguish, liberation from anguish is the Eightfold Path.

far beyond delusive thinking, right here is
    Nirvana.
san ze shō butsu e han-nya ha ra mi ta
All Buddhas of past, present, and future live by
    Prajñā Pāramitā
ko toku a noku ta ra sam-myaku sam-bo dai
attaining Anuttara-samyak-sambodhi.
ko chi han-nya ha ra mi ta
Therefore know that Prajñā Pāramitā
ze dai jin shū ze dai myō shū
is the great sacred mantra, the great vivid mantra,
ze mu jō shū ze mu to to shū
the unsurpassed mantra, the supreme mantra,
no jō is-sai ku shin jitsu fu ko
which completely removes all anguish. This is
    truth, not mere formality.
ko setsu han-nya ha ra mi ta shu
Therefore set forth the Prajñā Pāramitā mantra,
soku setsu shu watsu
set forth this mantra and proclaim:
gya tei gya tei ha ra gya tei hara so gya tei
Gaté gaté paragaté parasamgaté
bo ji sowa ka han-nya shin gyō
Bodhi svāhā![7]

---

[7] Daisetz T. Suzuki translates the next to last line as "Gone, gone, gone to the
other shore, landed at the other shore." The final word is an exclamation of joy.

Shō Sai Myō Kichijō Darani
The Dhārani of Good Fortune that
Averts Calamities

Recited after the "Heart Sutra" in most services.

> *No mo san man da moto nan*
> *ohara chi kotosha sono nan*
> *to ji to en gya gya gya ki gya ki un nun*
> *shifu ra shifu ra hara shifu ra hara shifu ra*
> *chishu sa chishu sa chishu ri chishu ri*
> *soha ja soha ja senchigya shiriei*
> *somo ko*

Tōrei Zenji: Bodhisattva's Vow

A homily by Tōrei Enji (1721–1792), recited after the first dedication during the service at sesshin. Originally in prose, it is set
in verse form to facilitate chanting.

Leader:

> *I am only a simple disciple,*
> *but I offer these respectful words:*

Assembly:

> *When I regard the true nature of the many dharmas,*[8]
> *I find them all to be sacred forms*
> *of the Tathāgata's never-failing essence.*
> *Each particle of matter, each moment,*

---

[8] Dharmas, with a lower case "d," can be read "phenomena."

is no other than the Tathāgata's inexpressible radiance.
With this realization, our virtuous ancestors,
with compassionate minds and hearts,
gave tender care to beasts and birds.
Among us, in our own daily lives,
who is not reverently grateful for the protections of life:
food, drink, and clothing!
Though they are inanimate things,
they are nonetheless the warm flesh and blood,
the merciful incarnations of Buddha.
All the more, we can be especially sympathetic
and affectionate with foolish people,
particularly with someone who becomes a sworn enemy
and persecutes us with abusive language.
That very abuse conveys the Buddha's boundless loving-
kindness.
It is a compassionate device to liberate us entirely
from the mean-spirited delusions we have built up
with our wrongful conduct from the beginningless past.
With our response to such abuse
we completely relinquish ourselves
and the most profound and pure faith arises.
At the peak of each thought a lotus flower opens,
and on each flower there is revealed a Buddha.
Everywhere is the Pure Land in its beauty.
We see fully the Tathāgata's radiant light
right where we are.
May we retain this mind
and extend it throughout the world
so that we and all beings
become mature in Buddha's wisdom.

Emmei Jikku Kannon Gyō
Ten Verse Kannon Sutra of Timeless Life

Recited at evening ceremonies on regular days, and during morning services at sesshin. A Rinzai sutra, it is also recited at some Sōtō centers in the West.

Kanzeon
Kanzeon!
namu butsu
I venerate the Buddha;
yo butsu u in
with the Buddha I have my source,
yo butsu u en
with the Buddha I have affinity —
buppō sō en
affinity with Buddha, Dharma, Sangha,
jōraku ga jō
constancy, ease, assurance, purity.
chō nen kanzeon
Mornings my thought is Kanzeon,
bō nen kanzeon
evenings my thought is Kanzeon,
nen nen jū shin ki
thought after thought arises in mind,
nen nen fu ri shin.
thought after thought is not separate from mind.

Hakuin Zenji: Song of Zazen

Dharma poem by Hakuin Ekaku (1685–1768). Recited during the ceremony at the end of the day during sesshin.

All beings by nature are Buddha,
as ice by nature is water;
apart from water there is no ice,
apart from beings no Buddha.
How sad that people ignore the near
and search for truth afar,
like someone in the midst of water
crying out in thirst,
like a child of a wealthy home
wandering among the poor.
Lost on dark paths of ignorance
we wander through the six worlds;
from dark path to dark path we wander,
when shall we be freed from birth and death?
For this the zazen of the Mahayana
deserves the highest praise:
offerings, Precepts, Pāramitās,
Nembutsu, atonement, practice —
the many other virtues —
all rise within zazen.
Those who try zazen even once
wipe away immeasurable crimes —
where are all the dark paths then?
the Pure Land itself is near.
Those who hear this truth even once
and listen with a grateful heart,
treasuring it, revering it,
gain blessings without end.

Much more, if you turn yourself about,
and confirm your own self-nature —
self-nature that is no nature —
you are far beyond mere argument.
The oneness of cause and effect is clear,
not two, not three, the path is straight;
with form that is no form,
going and coming — never astray;
with thought that is no thought
singing and dancing are the voice of the Law.
Boundless and free is the sky of Samādhi,
bright the full moon of wisdom,
truly is anything missing now?
Nirvana is right here, before our eyes,
this very place is the Lotus Land,
this very body the Buddha.

The Dedications and the Evening Message

Dedications are recited by the leader, with the assembly joining at the indented portions.

First Sutra Service Dedication

Recited after the "Heart Sutra" and "Shō Sai Myō Kichijō Darani" during the morning service at sesshin.

Buddha nature pervades the whole universe,
existing right here now.
With our reciting of "The Great Prajñā Pāramitā Heart
Sutra" [or] "Maka Hannya Haramita Shin Gyō"
and the "Shō Sai Myō Kichijō Darani,"

let us unite with:
The Ancient Seven Buddhas, Dai Oshō,
Shākyamuni Buddha, Dai Oshō,
Bodhidharma, Dai Oshō,
Tōzan Ryōkai, Dai Oshō,
Dōgen Kigen, Dai Oshō,
Keizan Jōkin, Dai Oshō,
Dai'un Sogaku, Dai Oshō,
Haku'un Ryōkō, Dai Oshō,
Kōun Zenshin, Dai Oshō; [9]
all founding teachers, past, present, future, Dai Oshō,
let true Dharma continue, Sangha relations become
complete;
all Buddhas throughout space and time,
all Bodhisattvas, Mahasattvas,
the great Prajñā Pāramitā.

Second Sutra Service Dedication

This dedication is read following "Tōrei Zenji: 'Bodhisattva's Vow'" and "Emmei Jikku Kannon Gyō" at the morning service during sesshin.

The Buddha and his teachers and his many sons and daughters
turn the Dharma wheel to show the wisdom of the stones and
clouds;
we dedicate the virtues of reciting "Tōrei Zenji's 'Bodhisattva's
Vow'" and the "Emmei Jikku Kannon Gyō" to:
Chōrō Nyogen, Dai Oshō,

---

[9] Key figures in the Sanbō Kyōdan lineage. The last three are Harada Dai'un Rōshi, Yasutani Haku'un Rōshi, and Yamada Kōun Rōshi.

Hannya Gempō, Dai Oshō,
Mitta Sōen, Dai Oshō,[10]
and to our relatives and companions of the past who rest
in deepest samādhi;
all Buddhas throughout space and time;
all Bodhisattvas, Mahasattvas;
The great Prajñā Pāramitā.

Sesshin Evening Service Dedication

Recited after "Hakuin Zenji: 'Song of Zazen' " during sesshin.

The sky of Samādhi and the moonlight of wisdom form the
*   temple of our practice;*
our friends and family members guide us as we walk the
*   ancient path;*
we dedicate the virtues of reciting "Hakuin Zenji's 'Song
*   of Zazen' " to:*
*   Rinzai Gigen Dai Oshō*
*   Hakuin Ekaku Dai Oshō*
and to the guardians of the Dharma and the protectors of
*   our sacred hall;*
*   all Buddhas throughout space and time;*
*   all Bodhisattvas, Mahasattvas;*
*   the great Prajñā Pāramitā.*

---

[10] These are Senzaki Nyogen Sensei, Yamamoto Gempō Rōshi, and Nakagawa Sōen Rōshi.

Sesshin Ending Dedication

Recited after the "Heart Sutra" in Sino-Japanese at the closing ceremony of sesshin. The assembly does not join in reading the names of ancestors.

> *In the purity and clarity of the Dharmakāya,*
> *in the fullness and perfection of the Sambhogakāya,*
> *in the infinite variety of the Nirmānakāya,*
> *we dedicate our sesshin and our reciting of*
> *Maka Hannya Haramita Shin Gyō to:*
>> *The Ancient Seven Buddhas, Dai Oshō,*
>> *Shākyamuni Buddha, Dai Oshō,*
>> *all Founding Teachers, past, present, future, Dai*
>> *Oshō;*
> *and for the enlightenment of bushes and grasses*
> *and the many beings of the world;* [11]
>> *all Buddhas throughout space and time;*
>> *all Bodhisattvas, Mahasattvas;*
>> *the great Prajñā Pāramitā.*

The Evening Message

Called out by the Jisha from just outside the dōjō during the ceremony at the end of the day of sesshin.

> *I beg to urge you everyone:*
> *life and death is a grave matter;*
> *all things pass quickly away.*

---

[11] At this point, special dedications to someone who is ill, or who has died, can be inserted.

> *Each of us must be completely alert;*
> *never neglectful, never indulgent.*

Daily Morning Service Dedication

Recited after the "Heart Sutra" and the "Shō Sai Myō Kichijō Darani" on ordinary days.

> *Our words ring out through space beyond the stars;*
> *their virtue and compassion echo back from all the many*
> *   beings;*
> *we recite "The Great Prajñā Pāramitā Heart Sutra [or]*
> *   Maka Hannya Haramita Shin Gyō" and the "Shō Sai*
> *   Myō Kichijō Darani"*
> *for renewal of the Buddha mind in fields and forests,*
> *homes and streets, throughout the world,*
> *in grateful thanks to all our many guides along the ancient*
> *   way;*
> *   all Buddhas throughout space and time;*
> *   all Bodhisattvas, Mahasattvas;*
> *   the great Prajñā Pāramitā.*

Daily Evening Service Dedication

Recited after the "Purification" and the "Emmei Jikku Kannon Gyō" on ordinary days.

> *Infinite realms of light and dark convey the Buddha mind;*
> *birds and trees and stars and we ourselves come forth in*
> *   perfect harmony;*
> *we recite our gāthā and our sutra for the many beings of*
> *   the world;*

in grateful thanks to all our many guides along the ancient
way;
    all Buddhas throughout space and time
    all Bodhisattvas, Mahasattvas;
    the great Prajñā Pāramitā.

Mealtime Sutras

Originally, Buddhist wayfarers ate only in the early morning and at noon, and this practice continues in Southern Buddhism. When the religion moved to a colder climate in China, a supper in the evening was added, but out of deference to tradition, it was called the "medicine stone," and consisted only of leftovers. In the Diamond Sangha, again out of deference to tradition (including rural American), the noon meal is called "dinner," and the evening meal "supper." Sutras are not recited for supper.

Meals are served formally to students as they sit in place in the dōjō, facing into the room, in a modified Sōtō ceremony, using bowls and chopsticks.

Sutras for Formal Meals

Verse on Opening the Bowls
Unopened bowls before everyone, hands at gasshō

    Buddha, born at Kapilavastu,
    attained the Way at Magadha,
    preached at Vārānashī,
    entered Nirvana at Kushinagara.
    Now as we spread the bowls of the Buddha Tathāgatha
    we make our vows together with all beings;
    we and this food and our eating are vacant.

Leader:

> *We take refuge in the Three Treasures,*
> *remembering our many honored guides*
> *with gratitude for their gifts of wisdom.*

The Ten Names of the Buddha

Participants spread their bowls. Servers enter during this recitation with trays of food and spoon out food into the bowls of students as they extend them in turn.

> *Vairochana, pure and clear Dharmakāya Buddha;*
> *Lochana, full and complete Sambhogakāya Buddha;*
> *Shākyamuni, infinitely varied Nirmānakāya Buddha;*
> *Maitreya, Buddha still to be born;*
> *all Buddhas everywhere, past, present, future;*
> *Mahayana Lotus of the Subtle Law Sutra;*
> *Mañjushrī, great wisdom Bodhisattva;*
> *Samantabhadra, great action Bodhisattva;*
> *Avalokiteshvara, great compassion Bodhisattva;*
> *all venerated Bodhisattvas, Mahāsattvas,*
> *The great Prajñā Pāramitā.*

Leader, at Breakfast:

> *Porridge is effective in ten ways*
> *To aid the student of Zen.*
> *No limit to the good result,*
> *Consummating eternal happiness.*

Leader, at Dinner:

> *These three virtues and six flavors*
> *are offered to the Buddha and Sangha;*
> *may all beings of the universe*
> *share alike this nourishment.*

The Spirit of Acceptance

> *First, we consider in detail the merit of this food and*
> *remember how it came to us;*
> *second, we evaluate our own virtue and practice, lacking or*
> *complete, as we receive this offering;*
> *third, we are careful about greed, hatred and ignorance, to*
> *guard our minds and to free ourselves from error;*
> *fourth, we take this good medicine to save our bodies from*
> *emaciation;*
> *fifth, we accept this food to achieve the Way of the*
> *Buddha.*

On Offering Food to Hungry Ghosts

A small dish is passed around, and each student offers a few grains
of rice, wheat, or barley, or a small bit of noodle or bread.

> *Oh, all you hungry ghosts,*
> *we now offer this food to you;*
> *may all of you everywhere*
> *share it with us together.*

On Lifting the Bowl of Rice in Gratitude

Bowls are held up at eye level. At the beginning of the last line,
everyone bows.

> The first portion is for the Three Treasures,[12]
> the second is for the Four Blessings,[13]

---

[12] The Buddha, the Dharma, and the Sangha.

[13] Teachers, parents, nation, and the many beings.

the third is for the Six Paths; [14]

together with all we take this food.

The first taste is to cut off all evil,

the second is to practice all good,

the third is to save the many; [15]

may we all attain the way of the Buddha.

On Washing the Bowls in Hot Tea

We wash our bowls in this water;

it has the flavor of ambrosial dew;

we offer it to all hungry ghosts;

may all be filled and satisfied.

At the End of the Meal

The world is like an empty sky;

the lotus does not adhere to water;

our minds surpassing that in purity,

we bow in veneration to the most exalted one.

The Verse for Informal Meals

This may be a translation of a Far Eastern gāthā. There are several English variations.

We venerate the Three Treasures

and are thankful for this meal,

---

[14] The Six Realms of devils, Hungry Ghosts, animals, titans, humans, and Devas.

[15] These three lines echo the Three Pure Precepts. See The Jukai Ceremony.

the work of many people
and the sharing of other forms of life.

The Jukai Ceremony

The Jukai ceremony is the initiation into the Buddha Way for the student of Zen Buddhism. It is the equivalent in Zen Buddhism for the Refuge Ceremony that is common to all Buddhism. It includes taking refuge in the Buddha, Dharma, and Sangha, and making vows to live by the light of the Three Pure Precepts and the Ten Grave Precepts of the Mahayana. Jukai is a ceremony for lay people, though it is also a part of priestly ordination. It is not a requirement for Zen Buddhist practice, but is offered as a ritual affirmation of oneself as a Buddhist wayfarer. Commonly students will renew their vows at Jukai Ceremonies every one or two years.

In the Diamond Sangha, the Jukai Ceremony is held at the end of the sesshin. The Rōshi seats himself before the altar facing the line of initiates, with a low table between them that holds a candle, flowers and incense. The assembly sits in a semi-circle around this group. The Rōshi begins with an explanation of procedures. Everybody then does three full bows and recites the "Purification" and the "Vandana" and "Ti-Sarana."

Rōshi's Introduction

Jukai is acceptance of the Precepts. It is the acknowledgment: "I am a disciple of the Buddha Shākyamuni." From this acceptance and acknowledgment arises practice on cushions and in daily life.

I take refuge in the Buddha, Dharma, and Sangha and find common ground with all Buddhists. I find my home in clear understanding, in wise teaching, and in the presence of beings about me.

I vow to keep all precepts, to practice all good dharmas, and to save the many beings — to be responsible as a disciple of the Buddha Shākyamuni. I take up the Ten Grave Precepts as guides in persevering with my responsibility.

I vow to realize, maintain, and convey the way of helping and not harming.

The Three Vows of Refuge

The Assembly Response is from a traditional Sōtō Zen Buddhist work that was revised by Dōgen Kigen under the title, *Kyōjūkai-mon, Doctrine of Jukai.*)[16] Initiates take turns reading their vows, beginning with the one sitting at the left-front corner facing the altar. With each response they repeat the traditional vow, and then they read the words they have composed as their own vow. After this set of vows, and the two subsequent sets, they make a full bow.

Rōshi: The Three Vows of Refuge.

Assembly: *The Great Precepts of all the Buddhas have been maintained and protected by all the Buddhas. Buddhas hand them down to Buddhas, and Ancestral Teachers hand them down to Ancestral Teachers. Acceptance and observance of the Precepts transcend past, present, and future, and form the perfect accord in realization between teacher and disciple, continuing through all ages.*

     Our great teacher Shākyamuni Buddha imparted them to Mahākāshyapa, and Mahākāshyapa transmitted them to Ānanda. Already the Precepts have passed through many generations in direct succession, reaching down to the present head of this temple.

---

[16] Robert Aitken, *The Mind of Clover: Essays in Zen Buddhist Ethics* (San Francisco: North Point Press, 1984), pp. 15, 180–81.

*Now, receiving the Great Precepts, I vow to requite my deep
obligation to the Buddhas and Ancestral Teachers. I pledge to
establish these Precepts as essential teachings for human beings and
other beings so that all will inherit the wisdom of the Buddha.*

Rōshi:	I take refuge in the Buddha.
Initiate:	I take refuge in the Buddha....
Rōshi:	I take refuge in the Dharma.
Initiate:	I take refuge in the Dharma....
Rōshi:	I take refuge in the Sangha.
Initiate:	I take refuge in the Sangha....

The Three Pure Precepts

The Assembly responses are from the *Kyōjūkaimon.*

Rōshi:	The Three Pure Precepts.
	I vow to maintain the Precepts.
Initiate:	I vow to maintain the Precepts....
Assembly:	*This is the cave whence all dharmas of all Buddhas arise.*
Rōshi:	I vow to practice all good dharmas.
Initiate:	I vow to practice all good dharmas....
Assembly:	*This is the path of fulfilled enlightenment.*
Rōshi:	I vow to save the many beings.
Initiate:	I vow to save the many beings....
Assembly:	*Transcending profane and holy, I liberate myself and others.*

The Ten Grave Precepts

The first Assembly Responses to the Precepts are comments commonly attributed to Bodhidharma from the book, *I-hsin Chieh-men
(Isshin Kaimon, The Precepts of One Mind)*, but probably this work

originates in the T'ien-tai school of Chinese Buddhism. The second Assembly Response is from the *Kyōjūkaimon.*[17]

Rōshi: The Ten Grave Precepts.
I take up the Way of Not Killing.

Assembly: *Self-nature is subtle and mysterious. In the realm of the everlasting Dharma, not giving rise to the idea of killing is called the Precept of Not Killing.*

Initiate: I take up the Way of Not Killing....

Assembly: *The Buddha seed grows in accordance with not taking life. Transmit the life of Buddha's wisdom and do not kill.*

Rōshi: I take up the Way of Not Stealing.

Assembly: *Self-nature is subtle and mysterious. In the realm of the unattainable Dharma, not having thoughts of gaining is called the Precept of Not Stealing.*

Initiate: I take up the Way of Not Stealing....

Assembly: *The self and things of the world are just as they are. The gate of emancipation is open.*

Rōshi: I take up the Way of Not Misusing Sex.

Assembly: *Self-nature is subtle and mysterious. In the realm of the ungilded Dharma, not creating a veneer of attachment is called the Precept of Not Misusing Sex.*

Initiate: I take up the Way of Not Misusing Sex....

Assembly: *The Three Wheels are pure and clear. When you have nothing to desire, you follow the way of all Buddhas.*

Rōshi: I take up the Way of Not Speaking Falsely.

Assembly: *Self-nature is subtle and mysterious. In the realm of the inexplicable Dharma, not preaching a single word is called the Precept of Not Speaking Falsely.*

Initiate: I take up the Way of Not Speaking Falsely....

Assembly: *The Dharma wheel turns from the beginning. There is neither surplus nor lack. The whole universe is moistened with nectar, and the truth is ready to harvest.*

---

[17] Ibid.

Rōshi: I take up the Way of Not Giving or Taking Drugs.

Assembly: *Self-nature is subtle and mysterious. In the realm of the intrinsically pure Dharma, not giving rise to delusions is called the Precept of Not Giving or Taking Drugs.*

Initiate: I take up the Way of Not Giving or Taking Drugs. . . .

Assembly: *Drugs are not brought in yet. Don't let them invade. That is the great light.*

Rōshi: I take up the Way of Not Discussing Faults of Others.

Assembly: *Self-nature is subtle and mysterious. In the realm of the flawless Dharma, not expounding upon error is called the Precept of Not Discussing Faults of Others.*

Initiate: I take up the Way of Not Discussing Faults of Others. . . .

Assembly: *In the Buddha Dharma, there is one path, one Dharma, one realization, one practice. Don't permit faultfinding. Don't permit haphazard talk.*

Rōshi: I take up the Way of Not Praising Myself while Abusing Others.

Assembly: *Self-nature is subtle and mysterious. In the realm of the equitable Dharma, not dwelling upon I against you is called the Precept of Not Praising Myself while Abusing Others.*

Initiate: I take up the Way of Not Praising Myself while Abusing Others. . . .

Assembly: *Buddhas and Ancestral Teachers realize the empty sky and the great earth. When they manifest the noble body, there is neither inside nor outside in emptiness. When they manifest the Dharma body, there is not even a bit of earth on the ground.*

Initiate: I take up the Way of Not Sparing the Dharma Assets. . . .

Assembly: *Self-nature is subtle and mysterious. In the genuine, all-pervading Dharma, not being stingy about a single thing is called the Precept of Not Sparing the Dharma Assets.*

Rōshi: I take up the Way of Not Sparing the Dharma Assets.

Assembly: *One phrase, one verse — that is the ten thousand things and one hundred grasses; one Dharma, one realization — that is all Bud-*

dhas and Ancestral Teachers. Therefore from the beginning, there has been no stinginess at all.

Rōshi: I take up the Way of Not Indulging in Anger.

Assembly: *Self-nature is subtle and mysterious. In the realm of the selfless Dharma, not contriving reality for the self is called the Precept of Not Indulging in Anger.*

Initiate: I take up the Way of Not Indulging in Anger. . . .

Assembly: *Not advancing, not retreating, not real, not empty. There is an ocean of bright clouds. There is an ocean of solemn clouds.*

Rōshi: I take up the Way of Not Defaming the Three Treasures.

Assembly: *Self-nature is subtle and mysterious. In the realm of the One, not holding dualistic concepts of ordinary beings and sages is called the Precept of Not Defaming the Three Treasures.*

Initiate: I take up the Way of Not Defaming the Three Treasures. . . .

Assembly: *The teishō of the actual body is the harbor and the weir. This is the most important thing in the world. Its virtue finds its home in the ocean of essential nature. It is beyond explanation. We just accept it with respect and gratitude.*

Verse of the Rakusu

The rakusu is a small, bib-like garment, which the students themselves sew in a "rice-field" pattern, the same pattern used in making the robes of Theravada monks and nuns, and the kesa worn as a formal garment by Mahayana priests. It is said that one day when the Buddha was standing with his disciples on a knoll overlooking rice fields, he was struck by the pattern they formed, and suggested that it be used to express the fecundity of the Dharma. At this point in the ceremony, the Rōshi explains about the rakusus which he is about to present to the initiates, each inscribed with the Dharma name they have selected for themselves in consultation with him. The Rōshi explains the meaning of the

Dharma names, presents the rakusus, and then he and the initiates
recite the "Verse of the Rakusu."

This same verse is recited in Sōtō assemblies at dawn when the
priests put on their kesas and lay people their rakusus. It is also
murmured privately when putting on the garment at other times.
It is the robe of the Buddha, and is treated respectfully and worn
on all religious occasions.

I wear the robe of liberation,
the formless field of benefaction,
the teachings of the Tathāgata,
saving all the many beings.

Dedication

After the "Verse of the Rakusu," the assembly recites the "Heart
Sutra" as the initiates and the Rōshi offer incense. This is followed by a dedication recited by the Rōshi, "Great Vows for All"
and final bows. The dedication can include special words for
people who are sick, or who have died.

At Magadha, at this very place,
deep into the sacred ground,
high into the empty sky,
broadly shading living things
the tree of wisdom thrives
by rain and soil and sunshine
and by your loving care that we maintain.
We dedicate the Prajñā Pāramitā Heart Sūtra,
our ceremony of Jukai, our sesshin, and ourselves
to you, Shākyamuni Buddha Dai Oshō,
we celebrate your sacred presence,
your boundless understanding, and your love.

Let your true Dharma continue,
and your Sangha relations become complete;
 all Buddhas throughout space and time;
 all Bodhisattvas, Mahasattvas,
 the great Prajñā Pāramitā.

THE SESSHIN

Daily Schedule

Periods of zazen are twenty-five minutes long, or perhaps less just before another event. Zazen periods are interspersed by kinhin, intervals of formal walking, when one also may step out and use the bathroom.

Dokusan (personal interviews) are held during periods of zazen and kinhin. Dokusan is voluntary, except during the morning of the first day, during the morning of the middle day (of seven-day sesshins), and during the morning of the last day — when everyone goes in order of seating. The last day ends with a closing ceremony that follows the formal interviews, usually ending about noon, followed by an informal lunch.

4:00 A.M.	Wake up, rise, and wash
4:15	Exercise

4:25	Tea
4:30	Zazen
4:50	Kentan (the Rōshi circumambulates the dōjō)
5:00	Zazen
6:30	Formal Breakfast
7:00	Maintenance work and rest
	Leaders' meeting
8:30	Sutra service
9:00	Zazen
9:40	Dokusan
11:30	Formal Dinner
12:00	Maintenance work and rest
1:30 P.M.	Tea
1:35	Zazen
2:00	Teishō
2:45	Zazen
3:20	Dokusan
4:30	Communal reading
5:00	Formal Supper
5:30	Maintenance work and rest
6:30	Zazen
7:10	Dokusan
8:50	Closing ceremony
9:00	Lights out

Leadership

The division of responsibilities of dōjō leaders in the Diamond Sangha has evolved in keeping with our circumstances as a lay center, first influenced by the Rinzai master Sōen Nakagawa, and then by Sanbō Kyōdan masters. Generally, the role of leaders working with the Rōshi is to serve as models and to keep things running smoothly so that the other students can set their ordinary concerns aside and devote themselves to their practice. Actually, every student has a leadership role during sesshin, though some roles are more demanding than others. The four main dōjō leaders, the cooks, and the mealtime and tea servers discharge their responsibilities during the formal practice; the others during the less formal intervals. Leaders will frequently fill in for and assist each other. The four dōjō leaders meet with the Rōshi briefly after breakfast each day during sesshin. The non-English terms are Sino-Japanese.

The *Rōshi* (Old Teacher) holds responsibility inherited in a direct line from the Buddha for the practice and welfare of the students and of the Sangha as a whole.

The *Tantō* (Head of the Line) is responsible for setting the tone of practice in the dōjō. She or he circumambulates the room periodically with the *kyōsaku*, "stick of encouragement" (used only by request in Diamond Sangha centers), and addresses the students briefly and extemporaneously twice a day, to hearten them in their practice.

The *Jisha* (Attendant) is in charge of dokusan proceedings, and serves as escort to the Rōshi coming and going from teishō. The Jisha is also responsible for such sesshin logistics as seating arrangements, the serving of meals, lighting, ventilation, visitors, and messages. She or he shares responsibility with the Head Resident for sesshin planning.

The *Ino* (Director of Labor) at Diamond Sangha centers leads the various services and ceremonies in the dōjō, including sutras in the morning, the three meals, tea ceremonies, and the sutras before and after the teishō.

The *Jikijitsu* (Regulator) is the timekeeper who sounds the various signals for wakeup, zazen, kinhin, teishō. She or he leads kinhin, and the early morning exercise.

A *Cook* is assigned for the same meal each day during sesshin. Preparation is made during the block of zazen before the meal, guided by a menu book.

Servers bring meals and tea to students in the dōjō. A head server leads and monitors these ceremonies.

Choppers prepare vegetables during the interval following breakfast, in accordance with the needs of the noon and supper cooks. A head chopper coordinates this work.

Two *Dishwashers* are assigned to each meal. They also put away the leftovers and clean up the kitchen.

Cleanup People are assigned to the dōjō, the dokusan room, the toilets, bedrooms, and grounds. They do their work in the interval after breakfast.

The *Flower Arranger* keeps the altars neat, arranges flowers and leaves, and renews the offerings.

The *Head Resident* shares responsibilities for sesshin planning with the Jisha. This job includes accepting reservations for the sesshin, making up the seating chart, and coordinating food buying.

The Three Essentials

Yasutani Haku'un Rōshi offered these three essentials, or guidelines, at the outset of every sesshin. They are empirically tested ways to help individual members become rooted and to find intimacy with essential nature, with other members, and with all beings.

> 1. *Keep the silence.* If a practice-related problem arises and it is necessary to discuss it, find a chance to speak quietly and privately to the Tantō about it, or mention it to the Rōshi in dokusan. If you have an urgent work-related or food-related problem, mention it quietly to your work leader or to the Jisha. Please don't speak or write notes to the cooks or to anyone else. Please don't seek counsel from or offer counsel to your fellow

students. Let the sesshin leaders and the Rōshi handle emergencies.

2. *Keep your eyes lowered.* Eye contact is distracting during sesshin. You are connecting with others at a deeper level anyway. Pay no attention to little irregularities in the schedule. Trust the leaders to be leaders.

3. *Let the sesshin flow.* Don't gesture to others. If two of you reach a door at the same time, simply allow one to precede and the other to follow. Limit your signals at meals and at tea to the appropriate gestures. Keep yourself contained.

DŌJŌ PERCUSSION
INSTRUMENTS

The names used for these instruments are from the Sino-Japanese.

The *Denshō* (Bell of the Hall) is a large bell, eighteen inches or more in height, suspended overhead just outside the dōjō. It is struck by the Jikijitsu with a long mallet for ten minutes before each block of zazen periods. The sequence includes three accelerandi — the blows coming faster and faster until they merge to a point — by which the students can tell how much time is left before the zazen begins.

The *Inkin* (Leadership Bell) is a handbell shaped like a small bowl, mounted on a handle. A metal striker is attached by a cord. The tone is high-pitched and penetrating. The Jikijitsu and the Ino each have an inkin, and use them to signal various events.

The *Han* (Board) is a thick rectangular wooden board, suspended by cords outside the dōjō and struck with a wooden mallet. It is used in ceremonies at the end of each day and of the sesshin. At smaller centers, it can substitute for the Denshō. Commonly the han is inscribed with the following traditional verse:

> *Completely freed from yes and no;*
> *great emptiness charged within;*
> *no questions, no answers;*
> *like a fish, like a fool.*

Kaihan (Opening the Board) is the act of striking the Han.

The *Shijō* (Cease and Be Quiet) bell is about nine inches high, struck by the Jikijitsu. Three bells signal the beginning of a period of zazen, two bells signal kinhin, and one bell signals that another event is about to begin.

The *Kanshō* (Shout Bell) is like the shijō bell, perhaps a bit larger. It is kept outside the dōjō near the head of the dokusan line and is used by the Jisha to signal the beginning and end of dokusan. In centers where possible disturbance of the neighbors is not a factor, the students will sound this bell in turn just before going to dokusan.

The *Keisu* (Gong) is a bronze bowl bell, twelve inches or more in height, struck by the Ino with a padded mallet to punctuate the chanting of the sutras.

The *Mokugyō* (Wooden Fish) is a hollow wooden drum, roughly spherical, carved as a stylized fish. It is struck on top with a mallet, and rests on a pad on the floor. The Ino plays it with a steady beat to keep time for sutra chanting.

The *Reitaku* (Hand Bell) is the Rōshi's bell which he rings at the end of each student's interview, signalling for the next student.

The *Suzu* (Bell) is the small hand bell rung through the halls as a wakeup call.

The *Taikō* (Great Drum) is used to announce the Rōshi's appearance in the dōjō for teishō and during the closing ceremony of sesshin.

The *Taku* (Clappers) are two pieces of hard wood, about two inches by two inches by ten inches. They are held parallel and struck together, making a sharp clack. The Jikijitsu uses them to lead kinhin, and the Ino also has a set with which to punctuate the mealtime sutras.

The *Umpan* (Cloud Plate) is a bronze plate shaped something like a fleur-de-lis. It hangs from cords in the kitchen, and is struck with a hard wooden mallet to produce a clangorous sound. The head server strikes it to signal mealtimes. It is also used in the ceremony at the end of sesshin.

A GLOSSARY OF BUDDHIST TERMS
AND USAGES

See also Syllabus: Zen Buddhist Sutra Book, The Sesshin: Leadership, and Dōjō Percussion Instruments; and the Bibliography. Japanese names are given in the traditional order, with surnames first. Most of the terms that are capitalized in definitions are also entries. For Mahayana read Mahayana Buddhist or Buddhism. For Zen read Zen Buddhist or Buddhism. For Rinzai or Sōtō read Rinzai or Sōtō Zen Buddhist or Buddhism. Note that Sanskrit terms that conventionally begin with Ś will be found under *Sh*. Abbreviations: c = century; C = Chinese; J = Japanese; P = Pali; S = Sanskrit.

Abhidharma, S; Abhidamma, P. Commentary on the Dharma. The collection of commentaries on Sutras. See Tripitaka.

Affinity. The tendency of Beings to come together as organisms, families, species, and other groupings, providing individuality and diversity within the Plenum.

Ahimsa, Ahimsā, S. Nonharming. Nurturing.

Amida, J. Amitābha.

Amitābha, S. Amida. The Buddha of Infinite Light and Life who saves Sentient Beings and presides over the Pure Land.

Ānanda (4th c. B.C.E.). One of the principal disciples of the Buddha Shākyamuni; the second Ancestral Teacher.

Ancestral Teachers. Teachers in the traditional Zen lineage. Founding Teachers, Patriarchs.

Ancient Seven Buddhas. The Buddha Shākyamuni and the six Buddhas who preceded him, according to Zen folklore.

Anger. An emotional response to something that is inappropriate or unjust. An emotion involved in self-protection. See Hatred.

Anguish. In Buddhism, painful resistance to the reality of mortality and dependence. See Duhkha.

Antinomianism, antinomian. In Buddhism: the notion that one can ignore the Precepts.

Anuttara-samyak-sambodhi, S. Supreme perfect enlightenment. Total unitive fulfillment.

Archetype. In Buddhism, a metaphor empowered by innate understanding and long-term usage. A legendary or historical figure who models an empowered metaphor and can be made one's own.

Arhat, S. One who has destroyed the obstacles to Nirvana; the Theravada ideal.

Avalokiteshvara, Avalokiteśvara, S. Sovereign Observer. Archetypal Bodhisattva of mercy. See Kanzeon.

Barrier. In Zen, a checkpoint, as at a frontier.

Beings. All entities that exist. Sentient Beings. See Many Beings.

Bodhi, S. Enlightenment.

Bodhi Tree. *Ficus religiosa.* The tree that sheltered the Buddha Shākyamuni before, during, and just after his Realization.

Bodhichitta, Bodhicitta, S. The aspiration for Enlightenment and Buddhahood.

Bodhidharma (6th c.). Semilegendary Indian or West Asian founder of Ch'an Buddhism; Archetype for steadfast Practice.

Bodhimanda, S. The spot or place under the Bodhi Tree where the Buddha Shākyamuni had his Realization. Dōjō.

Bodhisattva, S. One on the Path to Enlightenment; one who is enlightened; one who enlightens others; a figure in the Buddhist pantheon.

Bodhisattva Precepts. See Precepts.

Bodhisattva's Vow. Bosatsu Gangyō Mon, J. A homily by Tōrei Enji. Distinguish from "Bodhisattva Vows." See Syllabus, The Zen Buddhist Sutra Book: "Great Vows for All" and "Tōrei Zenji: 'Bodhisattva's Vow.' "

Body and Mind Dropped Away. The Self forgotten in Zazen or other activity.

Bonnō, J. Klesha.

Brahma Vihāra, S. Sublime Abode. The four progressive Brahma Vihāras are Maitrī, boundless loving-kindness; Karunā, boundless compassion; Mudita, boundless joy in the liberation of others; and Upekshā, boundless equanimity.

Buddha, S. Enlightened One. Shākyamuni. An enlightened person. A figure in the Buddhist pantheon. Any Being.

Buddha Dharma, S. The teaching of the Buddha Shākyamuni and his successors; Dharma; Buddhism; the Eightfold Path; Buddha Tao or Way.

Buddha Nature. Essential, Self, or True Nature.

Buddha Tao or Way. Buddha Dharma. The Eightfold Path.

Buddhahood. Enlightenment and compassion. The condition of a Buddha.

Cause-and-Effect. One explanation of Karma.

Chain of Causation. See Twelve-linked Chain of Causation.

Ch'an, C. Zen.

Chao-chou Ts'ung-sheng (778–897). Jōshū Jūshin, J. An especially revered Chinese Ch'an master.

Cheng-tao ke, C; *Shōdōka*, J. *Song of Realizing the Way*, a long Dharma poem by Yung-chia Hsüan-chüeh (665–713).*

Confirmation. In Zen, affirmation of Realization by one's teacher. Experientially, Realization is itself Confirmation.

Cross Over. Pāramitā; Save; transform.

Dai Oshō, J. Great priest, a posthumous honorific.

Daishi, J. Great Master, a posthumous title.

Dāna, S. Charity, giving, relinquishment (and their perfections). The First Pāramitā.

Darani, J. Dhāranī.

Dedication. Ekō, J. Turning. Transferring one's Merit to another. Transferring the Merit of a Sutra recitation to Buddhas, Bodhisattvas, Ancestral Teachers, etc.

Denominator (coinage by Yamada Kōun). The aspect of Essential Nature, underlying and infusing all things. See Numerator.

Dependent arising (also, co-dependent arising). Mutual Interdependence.

Deva, S. Heavenly being.

Dhāranī, S; Darani, J. A poetical invocation of praise.

Dharma, S. Religious, secular, or natural law; the Law of Karma; Buddha Dharma or Tao; teaching; the Dharmakāya. With a lower-case "d": a phenomenon or thing.

Dharma Gates. Incidents or Particulars that can enable one's Realization.

Dharma Wheel. The evolution of the Buddha Dharma in universal consciousness. See Turning the Dharma Wheel.

Dharmakāya, S. See Three Bodies of the Buddha.

Dhātu, S. Whatever is differentiated. The Eighteen Dhātus are the six senses: eye, ear, nose, tongue, body, and mind; the six fields sensed: form, sound, smell, taste, the tangible, and thought; six qualities of consciousness: seeing, hearing, smelling, tasting, feeling, and thinking.

---

* Sheng-yen, *The Sword of Wisdom: Lectures on "The Song of Enlightenment"* (Elmhurst, N.Y.: Dharma Drum Publications, 1990).

Dhyāna, S. Focused meditation and its form. Zazen, Zen. See Samādhi.

Diamond Sutra. The *Vajrachedikā Sutra,* S, a text of the Prajñā Pāramitā literature that stresses freedom from concepts.

Discursive (Western usage). Explanatory, prosaic, not clearly Presentational.

Dōgen Kigen (1200–1253). Venerated as the Japanese founder of the Sōtō tradition.

Dōjō, J. Bodhimanda. The training hall or Zendō. One's own place of Realization.

Dokusan, J. Sanzen. To work alone; personal interview with the Rōshi during formal Practice.

Duhkha, S. Anguish; a response to mortality and dependence. The consequences of denying that reality. The first of the Four Noble Truths.

Ego. In Buddhism, self-image. Self. Distinguish from egocentricity.

Eightfold Path. The ideals and Practice of Right Views, Right Thoughts, Right Speech, Right Conduct, Right Livelihood, Right Effort or Life-style, Right Recollection, and Right Absorption (in keeping with the insubstantial nature of the Self, Mutual Interdependence, and the sacred nature of each Being). The way of freeing oneself from Duhkha. The fourth of the Four Noble Truths.

Emptiness, Empty. The insubstantial nature of the Self and all selves. Realized as the same as substance.

Engaged Buddhism (coinage by Thich Nhat Hanh). Taking the Path, especially as a community. Practice within or alongside poisonous systems.

Engaku Monastery. Rinzai monastery in Kamakura, Japan.

Enlightenment. Bodhi. The ideal condition of Realization.

Essential Nature. The pure and clear Void that is charged with potential. The Denominator of Phenomena or Beings. Self Nature, True Nature, Buddha Nature.

Evil. Harmful, destructive. Distinguish from immoral.

Five Modes of the Particular and the Universal. A poetical work by Tung-shan Liang-chieh that recaps the insights of Zen Practice.* See Tōzan Ryōkai.

Forgetting the Self. Body and Mind Dropped (or Fallen) Away. The experience of everything disappearing with an act or with something sensed. Might be confirmed as Realization.

Founding Teachers. Ancestral Teachers.

Four Abodes. Brahma Vihāras.

Four Blessings. Teachers, parents, nation, and the Many Beings.

Four Noble Truths. Anguish is everywhere; there is a cause of anguish; there is liberation from anguish; liberation is the Eightfold Path. The basic Buddhist teaching.

Fudō, J; Acala, S. Immobile. Archetype of perseverance in the flames of hell. A reflex of the Buddha Vairochana.

Gasshō, J; Añjali, S. The Mudrā of hands held palm to palm before the lower part of the face, in devotion, in gratitude, or as a greeting.

Gateless. Completely open.

Gāthā, S. A four-line verse that sums up an aspect of the Dharma. In the Mahayana, it is often a Vow.

General Kuan. Kuan-yü (3rd c.), Chinese warrior later canonized as the God of War.

Goddess of Mercy. Kanzeon, Kuan-yin.

Great (Ball of) Doubt. Total absorption in inquiry. See Red-Hot Iron Ball.

Greed. Affinity exploited to serve the self. The first of the Three Poisons.

Hakuin Ekaku (Zenji) (1685–1768). Japanese Rinzai master, ancestor of all contemporary Rinzai teachers.

Harada Dai'un or Sogaku (1870–1961). Japanese Zen founder of the syncretic school that became the Sanbō Kyōdan. Teacher of Yasutani Haku'un and of Westerners.

---

* William F. Powell, *The Record of Tung-shan* (Honolulu: University of Hawaii Press, 1986), pp. 61–63.

Harmony. Mutual Interdependence realized.

Hatred. Indulging or dwelling in Anger. The second of the Three Poisons.

Heart Sutra. Prajñā Pāramitā Hrdaya Sūtra, S; *Hannya Haramita Shin Gyō*, J. A brief summary of the Mahayana, stressing the complementarity of substance and emptiness. (See Syllabus, The Zen Buddhist Sutra Book.)

Hinayana, Hinayāna, S. Small Vehicle (pejorative); schools of Classical or Southern Buddhism, of which only Theravada survives.

Hotei, J. The so-called Laughing Buddha, associated wtih Maitreya. A god of good fortune.

Hsin-hsin ming, C; *Shinjinmei*, J. *Precepts of Faith in Mind*, a long Dharma poem attributed to the Third Chinese Ancestor, Seng-ts'an (d. 606).*

Hsüan-tang (660/2–664). Chinese Buddhist master who translated important sutras he himself collected in India.

Hua-yen Ching or *Hua-yen Sūtra*. Chinese version of the *Avatamsaka Sūtra*, which stresses the Particularity of all beings, and their innate Harmony.†

Hui-neng, C (638–713). Sixth Ancestral Teacher. Traditionally the key figure in Ch'an Buddhist acculturation.

Hungry Ghosts. Preta, S. Ravenous beings with distended bellies and tiny throats. See Six Realms.

Ignorance. Neglecting or ignoring Essential Nature, the primal harmony of Beings, and their sacredness. The third of the Three Poisons. Distinguish from Not Knowing.

Interbeing (coinage by Thich Nhat Hanh). The Sambhogakāya. The many as the self or the particular, the dynamics of that reality, and its experience.

---

* Shen-yen, *Faith in Mind: A Guide to Ch'an Practice* (Elmhurst, N.Y.: Dharma Drum Publications, 1987).

† Thomas Cleary, trans., *The Flower Ornament Scripture: A Translation of the Avatamsaka Sutra*, 3 vols. (Boulder: Shambhala, 1984–87).

Intimacy. In Zen, the nature of Practice and its experience.

Jizō, J.; Kshitigarbha, S. Earth-treasury or Earth-womb; Archetypal Bodhisattva who saves living and dead children, wayfarers, fishermen, and people in hell.

Jukai, J. The ceremony of accepting the Buddha as one's teacher and the Precepts as guides. (See Syllabus, The Zen Buddhist Sutra Book; Jukai Ceremony.)

Kalpa, S. A particular eon. An immeasurably long period of time.

Kannon, Kanzeon, J. Kuan-yin.

Kanzeon, Kannon, J. Kuan-yin. One who hears the sounds of the world; the Archetypal Bodhisattva of mercy. Derived from Avalokiteshvara.

Karma, S. Action. Cause-and-effect; affinity; the function of Mutual Interdependence. Distinguish from fate.

Karunā, S. See Brahma Vihāra.

Keisaku, J. Kyōsaku.

Keizan Jōkin (1268–1325). Japanese great-grandson in the Dharma of Dōgen Kigen, compiler of the *Denkōroku*, J *(Transmission of Light)*.*

Kenshō, J. Seeing (True) Nature. Realization. See Satori.

Kentan, J. Viewing the rows; the circumambulation of the Dōjō by the Rōshi or a Dōjō leader.

Kesa, J. A robe worn over the usual robe on formal occasions by Mahayana monks and nuns, patterned after the traditional single square of cloth worn by the Buddha.

Kinhin, J. Walking verification. Sutra walk. The formal walk between periods of zazen.

Klesha, Kleśa, S; Bonnō, J. Afflictions, obstacles. The Three Poisons.

Knowledge. Formulated Wisdom.

Kōan, J. Universal/Particular. A presentation of the harmony of

---

* Thomas Cleary, *Transmission of Light* (San Francisco: North Point Press, 1990).

the Universal and the Particular; a theme of Zazen to be made clear. A classic Mondō, or Zen story.

Koko An, J. "The Little Temple Here"; Diamond Sangha temple in Manoa Valley, Honolulu.

Kuan-yin, C. Kanzeon Kannon.

Kumārajīva (344–413). Central Asian Buddhist master instrumental in translating important Buddhist texts into Chinese.

Kyōsaku or Keisaku, J. Stick of encouragement carried by a Dōjō leader and applied to the shoulders upon request to stimulate concentration.

Laughing Buddha. Hotei.

Law of Karma. The way things act. Karma. Cause-and-effect, Affinity, Mutual Interdependence.

Layman P'ang. P'ang-yün, C (740–808); Hō Koji, J. Lay Ch'an disciple memorialized in the *Recorded Sayings of the Layman P'ang.* *

Life-and-Death or Birth-and-Death. Samsāra; the realm of transience, relativity, and Karma.

Lochana, S. The body or person of Vairochana, incarnating Harmony, Interbeing, the Sangha, and the Sambhogakāya.

Lotus Land. Nirvana. Pure Land.

Lotus of the Subtle Law Sūtra. Saddharma Pundarika Sūtra, S. Teachings of the Middle Way in parables.†

Mahākāshyapa, Mahākāśyapa (4th c. B.C.E.). Principal heir of the Buddha Shākyamuni. The first Ancestral Teacher.

Mahāparinirvāna Sūtra, S. The account of the Buddha Shākyamuni's last days, his last teachings, and his death.‡

---

* Ruth Fuller Sasaki et al., *The Recorded Sayings of the Layman P'ang: A Ninth Century Classic* (New York: Weatherhill, 1971).

† Bunnō Katō et al., trans., *The Threefold Lotus Sutra* (New York: Weatherhill, 1975).

‡ Kosho Yamamoto, trans., *Mahaparinirvana-sutra: A Complete Translation from the Classical Chinese,* 3 vols. (Ube-shi Yamaguchi-ken: Karinbunko, 1973–75). Distinguish from the shorter Theravada text: "Mahāparinibbāna Sūtra," Maurice Walshe, trans., *Thus I Have Heard: The Long Discourses of the Buddha* (London: Wisdom Publications, 1987), pp. 231–90.

Mahāsattva, S. Great noble being.

Mahayana, Mahāyāna, S. Great Vehicle; the Buddhism of East Asia, also found in Vietnam. Tibetan Buddhism is often considered to be Mahayana. The Practice of saving the many Beings.

Maitreya, S. The Compassionate One; the future, potential, or inherent Buddha.

Maitrī, S. See Brahma Vihāra.

Makyō, J. Uncanny realm; a deep dream of participation in the Buddha Dharma.

Mani, S. Talisman pearl; the jewel or pearl of Buddhahood.

Mañjushrī, Mañjuśrī, S. Beautiful Virtue; Archetypal Bodhisattva of Wisdom.

Mantra, S. A spell; an empowered phrase or text.

Many Beings. Shujō, J. All Beings. Distinguish from Sentient Beings.

Māra. The destroyer; the Evil One.

Maudgalyāyana (4th c. B.C.E.). Prominent disciple of the Buddha Shākyamuni.

Merit. The good results of good action. A function of Karma and Mutual Interdependence.

Metaphor. A Presentation of something in terms of another, expressing their unity. In Buddhism, any Presentation.

Mettā. P. Concern for the welfare of others. Loving-kindness, Maitrī. See Brahma Vihāra.

Middle Way. The Way of the Buddha, harmonizing the Particular and the Universal, Cause-and-Effect, Essential Nature and Phenomena, the Three Bodies of the Buddha, etc. The Eightfold Path.

Mind. The unknown and unknowable that comes forth as the Plenum with its particular Beings and their interdependence and affinities. Essential Nature. Also the human mind.

Mind Mirror. That which presents, or the one who presents, the Mind.

Mind Road. The incessant, troublesome sequence of thoughts.

Mindfulness, Mindful. Attention. Attention to the breath. Right Recollection of the Self and others as insubstantial, interdependent, and sacred. See Eightfold Path.

Mondō, J. Question and answer; a Zen dialogue intended to strike sparks of the Dharma. See Kōan.

Morality, moral. Refers to the process of character formation and the state of personal nobility. Pursued on the Eightfold Path and fulfilled in the Pāramitās.

Mu, J; Wu, C. No; does not have. A kōan from Case I of *Wu-men kuan.*

Mudita, S. See Brahma Vihāra.

Mudrā, S. A seal or sign; hand or finger position or gesture that presents an aspect of the Dharma.

Mutual Interdependence. Dependent arising. The function and dynamics of Interbeing.

Nakagawa Sōen (1907–1984). Japanese Zen master of Ryūtaku Monastery; teacher of Westerners.

Nembutsu, J. Recalling Buddha. The Pure Land school practice of repeating "Namu Amida Butsu," "Veneration to the Buddha Amitābha."

Net of Indra. A model of the Plenum found in the *Hua-yen Ching.* Each point in the net perfectly contains all the points.

Nirmanakāya, S. See Three Bodies of the Buddha.

Nirvana, Nirvāna, S. Extinction of craving; liberation found in Practice and Realization. See Pure Land.

Noble, Nobility. In Buddhism, keeping the Buddha Dharma.

Not Knowing. Accepting the fact of mystery as the essence.

Numerator (coinage by Yamada Kōun). The Phenomenal aspect. See Denominator.

Ōbaku Zen Buddhism. A Rinzai school that includes elements of Pure Land practice. Distinguish from teachings of Huang-po Hsi-yün (Ōbaku Ki'un).

Pāramitā, S. Cross Over (to the shore of Nirvana). Save; transform. Perfection as condition or Practice. The Six Pāramitās are the ideals of giving, morality, forbearance, vitality, focused

meditation, and wisdom. Another enumeration, The Ten
Pāramitās, adds skillful means, resolve, strength, and knowledge.

Particularity or Particular. In Zen: the quality of a Phenomenon
or a Being.

Path. The Eightfold Path. Tao, Way, Buddha Dharma.

Patriarchs. Ancestral Teachers.

Perfection. See Pāramitā.

Phenomena, Phenomenon. Beings, a Being. The Numerator of
Essential Nature.

Platform Sutra of the Sixth Ancestor. Liu-tsu T'an-ching, C; *Rokuso
Dankyō,* J.* Memorializes Hui-neng.

Plenum. The Universe and its Many Beings. Realized as the Void.

Practice. Shugyo, J. Austerities, training. Endeavors in the Dōjō;
Zazen. To take the Eightfold Path; to follow the Precepts; to
Turn the Dharma Wheel.

Practice Period. Training Period.

Prajñā (Pāramitā), S. Wisdom, Enlightenment, or Bodhi (and its
perfection).

Pratyeka, S. Self-enlightened. One who lives and is enlightened
alone. See Shrāvaka, Bodhisattva.

Precepts. In Mahayana, the Sixteen Bodhisattva Precepts are: The
Three Vows of Refuge in the Three Treasures; the Three Pure
Precepts of avoiding evil, practicing good, and saving the Many
Beings; and the Ten Grave Precepts of not killing, not stealing,
not misusing sex, not speaking falsely, not giving or taking
drugs, not discussing faults of others, not praising oneself while
abusing others, not sparing the Dharma assets, not indulging
in anger, and not defaming the Three Treasures. (See Syllabus,
The Zen Buddhist Sutra Book: Jukai Ceremony.)

Presentation, Presentational (Western usage). A Particular expression or appearance without Discursive explanation.

---

* Philip B. Yampolsky, *The Platform Sutra of the Sixth Patriarch: The Text of the Tun-
huang Manuscript* (New York: Columbia University, 1967).

Pure Land. Nirvana; the afterlife envisioned in the Pure Land schools of Buddhism. Lotus Land. Realized as this very place.

Pure Land Buddhism. Faith in the saving power of the Buddha Amitābha.

Raihai, J. Prostration before the altar or the Rōshi.

Realization. Genjō, J. Actualization. A glimpse of empty or unitive possibilities. Prajñā experienced through one of the senses, acknowledged by a confirmed teacher. Made true for oneself, Kenshō. Understanding, Confirmation.

Rebirth. The coherent, changing karma of an individual or a cluster of individuals reappearing after death. The continuous arising of coherent, changing karma during life. Distinguish from Reincarnation.

Red-Hot Iron Ball. A physical sensation of Great Doubt.

Reincarnation. The notion that an enduring self reappears after death in a new birth. Distinguish from Rebirth.

Right Recollection. Mindfulness of ephemerality, Interbeing, and the sacred nature of all things. See Mindfulness, Eightfold Path.

Rinzai Gigen, Lin-chi I-hsüan (d. 866), venerated as the Chinese founder of the Lin-chi (Rinzai) tradition.

Rinzai Zen Buddhism. Today, the Zen sect in which Kōan study is used in conjunction with Zazen.

Rōshi, J. Old teacher. Now the title of the confirmed Zen teacher.

Ryūtaku Monastery. Zen Monastery in Mishima, Japan.

Sage. In Buddhism, an enlightened, compassionate person. A Buddha.

Samādhi, S. Absorption. The quality of Zazen. One with the Universe. See Dhyāna.

Samantabhadra, S. Pervading Goodness. Archetypal Bodhisattva of great action (in Turning the Dharma Wheel).

Sambhogakākaya, S. See Three Bodies of the Buddha.

Samsāra, S. The rising and falling of Life-and-Death. The relative world, realized as the same as Nirvana.

Samu. Work ceremony. Temple maintenance as part of formal Practice.

Sanbō Kyōdan. Order of the Three Treasures. A lay Japanese Sōtō tradition that includes elements of Rinzai practice, founded by Yasutani Haku'un in Kamakura, Japan.

Sangha, S. Aggregate. Buddhist community; any community, including that of all Beings.

Sanzen, J. Dokusan.

Satori, J. Prajñā. Enlightenment; the condition or (sometimes) the experience of Enlightenment. See Realization, Kenshō.

Save. In Buddhism, enable or help (someone) to Cross Over. Transform (someone or something) for the better.

Self. In Buddhism, the insubstantial individual that is nonetheless unique and sacred.

Self-nature. The essential quality of the Self. True Nature, Essential Nature, Buddha Nature.

Sentient Beings. Ujō, J. Beings with senses. Human beings.

Senzaki Nyogen (1876–1958). First Japanese Zen teacher to settle in the West; a disciple of Shaku Sōen Zenji.

Sesshin, J. To touch, receive, and convey the Mind; the intensive Zen retreat of three to seven days.

Seven Buddhas. See Ancient Seven Buddhas.

Shaku Sōen (Zenji) (1859–1919). Japanese Master of Engaku Monastery in Kamakura. He introduced Zen to the West at the World Parliament of Religions in Chicago in 1892.

Shākyamuni, Śākyamuni, S. Sage of the Shākya Clan; the historical Buddha (5th–4th c. B.C.E.). Founder of Buddhism. Archetype of Prajñā, Karunā, and the Nirmānakāya.

Shamantha, Śamantha, S. Concentration. The Chinese translate it by its mental function: Stopping. The meditative practice of stillness that reveals the insubstantial nature of the self.

Shāriputra, Śāriputra, S. (4th c. B.C.E.). A prominent heir of the Buddha Shākyamuni; interlocutor in the "Heart Sutra."

Shasu, J. The Mudrā of hands held over each other across the solar plexus; used during kinhin and at other times in the temple, encouraging Right Recollection.

Shikan, J. Shamantha/Vipashyanā. The meditation of the Tendai school. See T'ien-ta'i, Shikantaza, Zazen.

Shikantaza, J. Body and Mind Dropped Away in Zazen.

Shīla, Śīla, S. Restraint. Morality. Practicing the Precepts.

Shintō, J. Way of the Gods. The indigenous religion of Japan. Distinguish from Shinshū, a form of Pure Land Buddhism.

Shōbōgenzō, J, *True Dharma Eye Treasury*, the collection of Dōgen's many essays on Zen and its practice.

Shōsan or Hossen, J. Dharma encounter. The formal, public equivalent of Dokusan.

Showing the Bowl (Western coinage). Presenting the Buddha Dharma in the world.

Shrāvaka, Śrāvaka, S. A disciple. One who is enlightened by the Buddha's teaching. See Pratyeka, Bodhisattva.

Shūnyatā, Śūnyatā, S. The Void that is charged with potential.

Shūrangama Sutra, Śūrangama Sūtra. The best-known sutra with this title is Chinese in origin. It sets forth the many delusions and the means for seeing through them.*

Sit, Sitting. Zazen.

Six Flavors (of food). Bitter, sweet, sour, peppery, salty, and neutral.

Six Modes of Being. Six Realms.

Six Paths. Six Realms.

Six Realms or Worlds. The realms of devils, Hungry Ghosts, animals, titans, human beings, and Devas, through which one is constantly transmigrating.

Sixteen Bodhisattva Precepts. See Precepts.

Sixth Ancestor or Patriarch. Hui-neng.

Skandha, S. Aggregate. The five Skandhas that make up the Self

---

* Charles Luk, trans., The *Śūrangama Sūtra* (*Leng Yen Ching*) (London: Rider, 1966).

are forms of the world, sensation, perception, formulation, and consciousness. Realized as Empty.

Sōdō, J. Monks' residence hall. Zendō.

Song of Zazen. Zazen Wasan, J. Dharma poem by Hakuin Ekaku.

Sōtō Zen Buddhism. Today, the Zen sect that uses Shikantaza as a principal practice in Zazen.

Sudden Enlightenment. Kenshō. Realization and its teaching.

Suffering. Enduring, allowing; enduring pain. Distinguish from Anguish. See Duhkha.

Sutra, Sūtra, S; Sutta, P. Sermons by the Buddha Shākyamuni and those attributed to him; Buddhist scripture. See Tripitaka.

Suzuki Daisetz (D. T. Suzuki) (1870–1966). Japanese lay disciple of Shaku Sōen; the scholar most responsible for the dissemination of knowledge about Zen in the West.

Suzuki Shunryū (1904–1971). Japanese Sōtō founder and first abbot of the Zen Center of San Francisco.

Taking Refuge. The ceremony of acknowledging the Buddha, Dharma, and Sangha as one's home, common to all Buddhist traditions. See Precepts, Jukai. (See also Syllabus, The Zen Buddhist Sutra Book: Jukai Ceremony.)

Takuhatsu, J; Pindapāta, S. Ceremonial acceptance of alms in the neighborhood of the temple.

Tan, J. Row; line of people doing zazen. Dōjō.

Tao, C. Way. Buddha Dharma; the Eightfold Path. Distinguish from the Tao of Taoism.

Tathāgata, S. One who comes forth (presenting Essential Nature with particular qualities). A Buddha. Shākyamuni.

Tea Woman (Western coinage). Refreshment-stand proprietor. An unnamed, enlightened woman.

Teishō, J. Presentation of the shout; the Dharma presented by the Rōshi in a public talk.

Ten Grave Precepts. See Precepts.

Ten Ways (that porridge is effective). It improves the complexion, quickens the spirit, lengthens life, promotes good digestion, refreshes the voice, feels light in the stomach, keeps the body healthy, satisfies hunger, quenches thirst, and maintains bodily regularity.

Tendai, J. T'ien-t'ai.

Theravada, Theravāda, S. Way of the Elders. Today, the Buddhism of South and Southeast Asia. See Hinayana.

Three Bodies (of the Buddha). The complementary natures of Buddhahood and the world: Dharmakāya, the Dharma or law body of Essential Nature; Sambhogakāya, the bliss body of Mutual Interdependence; and Nirmānakāya, the transformation body of uniqueness and variety.

Three Poisons. Greed, Hatred, and Ignorance: the main kinds of self-centeredness that hinder the Practice. See Klesha.

Three Pure Precepts. See Precepts.

Three Treasures or Jewels. The Buddha, Dharma, and Sangha; Enlightenment, the Way, and community: the basic elements of Buddhism.

Three Virtues (of rice). Well cooked; pure and clean; prepared with the correct attitude in accordance with the rules.

Three Vows of Refuge. See Taking Refuge, Jukai, Precepts.

Three Worlds. Realms of consciousness: desire, form, and no form — that is, attachment, acceptance, and transcendence. Also past, present, and future.

T'ien-t'ai, C; Tendai, J. Early school of Chinese Buddhism that includes scholastic, devotional, esoteric, and meditative teachings. An antecedent of subsequent schools.

Tōrei Enji (Zenji) (1721–1792). Japanese Dharma heir of Hakuin Ekaku; de facto founder of Ryūtaku Monastery.

Tōzan Ryōkai, J. Tung-shan Liang-chieh (807–869), venerated as the Chinese founder of Ts'ao-tung (Sōtō).

Training Period. Ango, J. Peaceful Dwelling. A seclusion of six weeks to four months that includes Sesshins. Practice Period.

Transmigrating. The process of Rebirth.

Transmission. Succession to the wisdom and compassion of the Buddha Shākyamuni and his heirs. Confirmation of such succession by a teacher with transmission.

Tripitaka, S. Three baskets; the three main teachings of Buddhism: the Sutras, the Vinaya, and the Abhidharma.

True Nature. Self, Essential, or Buddha Nature.

Ts'ao-ch'i, C. Hui-neng's temple. Hui-neng.

Turning the Dharma Wheel. Lending wisdom and energy to the transformational process of the Buddha Dharma in the world. See Practice, Engaged Buddhism.

Turning Word. A skillful, appropriate expression that can prompt Realization. See Upāya.

Twelve-linked Chain of Causation. The classical karmic cycle: Ignorance conditions karmic-formations, which condition consciousness, which conditions mind-and-body, which conditions the six sense organs, which condition contact, which conditions feeling, which conditions craving, which conditions grasping, which conditions becoming, which conditions birth, which conditions aging and death. With no liberation from this chain, it is endlessly repeated.

Unborn. Essential nature, which does not come or go.

Understanding. Stepping under and taking on oneself. Knowing.

Universe. The Plenum. The Void.

Upāya, S. Skillful, appropriate means in Turning the Dharma Wheel, or prompting Realization.

Upekshā, S. See Brahma Vihāra.

Vairochana, Vairocana, S. The Sun Buddha; Archetype of Bodhi, total purity, and the Dharmakāya.

Vajrayana, Vajrayāna, S. The Way of the Adamantine Truth; Tibetan Buddhism.

Vimalakīrti, S. Semilegendary lay disciple of the Buddha Shākyamuni, memorialized in the *Vimalakīrti Nirdesha Sūtra*. Part of the Prajñā Pāramitā literature, this sutra seeks to spell out a reconciliation of the dichotomies of form and emptiness.*

---

* Charles Luk, trans., *The Vimalakīrti Nirdeśa Sutra* (Boston: Shambhala, 1990); Robert A. F. Thurman, *The Holy Teachings of Vimalakīrti: A Mahayana Scripture* (University Park: Pennsylvania State University Press, 1976).

Vinaya, S. The moral teachings. See Tripitaka.

Vipashyanā, Vipaśyanā, S; Vipassanā, P. Insight. The meditative practice of seeing into the insubstantial nature of the self and its sensations, thoughts, and emotions.

Void. Shūnyatā. Vast Emptiness that is full of potential. See Mind, Dharmakāya. Realized as the Plenum.

Vow. Usually, the expression of resolve to attain Buddhahood and that all beings attain it. See Bodhichitta.

Way. Tao, Dharma.

Wisdom. Prajñā. Realization and its insights.

Wu-men Hui-K'ai, C (1183–1260); Mumon Ekai, J. Chinese master, compiler of *The Gateless Barrier*.

Yamada Kōun or Zenshin (1907–1989). Japanese master of the Sanbō Kyōdan; teacher of Westerners.

Yamamoto Gempō (1866–1961). Japanese Rinzai master of Ryūtaku Monastery; teacher of Nakagawa Sōen.

Yasutani Haku'un or Ryōkō (1895–1973). Japanese founder of the Sanbō Kyōdan; teacher of Yamada Kōun and of Westerners.

Yaza, J. Night zazen.

Zazen, J. The practice of seated, focused meditation; formal Zen practice. Dhyāna.

Zen, J. Focused meditation; the Zen tradition. Derived from Ch'an and Dhyāna.

Zendō, J. Zen hall; Zen center. Dōjō.

Zenji, J. Zen master, usually a posthumous honorific.

AN ANNOTATED BIBLIOGRAPHY

Introductions to Zen Buddhist Practice

1. Robert Aitken, *Taking the Path of Zen* (San Francisco: North Point Press, 1982). Methods and modes of zazen: pp. 3–25; the kōan Mu: pp. 95–109.

2. Philip Kapleau, *The Three Pillars of Zen: Teaching, Practice, and Enlightenment* (Boston: Beacon Press, 1965). The syncretic path of Yasutani Haku'un Rōshi. Verbatim interviews with Western students: pp. 96–154; realization stories, pp. 204–68.

3. Shunryū Suzuki, *Zen Mind, Beginner's Mind* (New York: Weatherhill, 1970). A graceful introduction to Sōtō Zen Buddhist practice. The basics of "pure sitting," pp. 21–45; the attitude of the Zen student: pp. 49–88.

4. Flora Courtois, *An Experience in Enlightenment* (Wheaton, Ill.:

Theosophical Press, 1986). A brief, personal account of the perennial path, culminating in a confirmed realization.

5. Nyogen Senzaki and Ruth Strout McCandless, *Buddhism and Zen* (San Francisco: North Point Press, 1987). Warmhearted comments by the first Japanese monk to settle outside the Japanese community in the United States. See especially pp. 3–20, 59–71.

6. Zenkei Shibayama, *A Flower Does Not Talk: Zen Essays* (Rutland, Vt.: Tuttle, 1970). Insightful comments on Hakuin Zenji's "Song of Zazen," pp. 63–140, and the "Six Oxherding Pictures," pp. 152–203.

The Enlightened World View

1. John Blofeld, *The Zen Teaching of Huang Po: On the Transmission of Mind* (New York: Grove Press, 1958). An awesome presentation of the vast, brilliant universe of Zen experience. See especially pp. 29–52.

2. Kazuaki Tanahashi, *Moon in a Dewdrop: Writings of Zen Master Dōgen* (San Francisco: North Point Press, 1985). Difficult but rewarding essays by the founder of Sōtō Zen Buddhism in Japan. Try the essay translated as "Actualizing the Fundamental Point," pp. 69–73, with help from the cogent explications found in Hee Jin Kim, *Dōgen Kigen: Mystical Realist* (Tucson: University of Arizona Press, 1987); check Kim's index, p. 317, under "Kōan, realized in life."

3. Ruth Fuller Sasaki, *The Recorded Sayings of Lin-chi Hui-chao of Chen Prefecture* (Kyoto: Institute for Zen Studies, 1975). The rigorous, often humorous sermons and dialogues of the founder of Rinzai Zen. The longer "Discourses," pp. 1–39, might be more instructive for the beginner than the more succinct dialogues elsewhere in the book.

4. Norman Waddell, *The Unborn: The Life and Teachings of Zen Master Bankei* (San Francisco: North Point Press, 1984). Zen

in daily life for lay people, very readable yet scholarly. The "Dialogues," pp. 116–51, might be a good place to start.

5. Arthur Braverman, *Mud and Water: A Collection of Talks by the Zen Master Bassui* (San Francisco: North Point Press, 1989). An accessible collection of dialogues with lay people and clerics. Profound common sense — see especially pp. 81–114.

6. Kazuaki Tanahashi, *Penetrating Laughter: Hakuin's Zen and Art* (Woodstock, N.Y.: Overlook Press, 1984). Profound yet often amusing dialogues; fascinating ink paintings, with cogent comments. Leaf through the paintings to begin with, pp. 33–89.

Anthologies

1. Thomas Cleary, *The Original Face: An Anthology of Rinzai Zen* (New York: Grove Press, 1978). Japanese Rinzai Zen writings, including those of Shidō Bunan, pp. 101–5; and Tōrei Enji, pp. 141–58.

2. Thomas Cleary, *Timeless Spring: A Soto Zen Anthology* (New York: Weatherhill, 1980). Includes the metaphysical poem by Shih-tou Hsi-ch'ien (Sekitō Kisen), "The Merging of Difference and Unity," pp. 36–39; and writings of Ts'ao-shan Pen-chi (Sōzan Honjaku), pp. 50–58.

3. Daisetz T. Suzuki, *Manual of Zen Buddhism* (New York: Grove Press, 1960). The classic anthology of Chinese and Japanese Zen writings, first published in 1935. Aldous Huxley is said to have chosen it as a book he would take along to a desert island. See especially the "Ten Oxherding Pictures," pp. 127–34, and plates II–XI.

English Commentaries on Kōans

For comparative purposes, see the sections on Case I of the *Wu-men-kuan*, in the pages noted.

1. Robert Aitken, *The Gateless Barrier: The Wu-men kuan (Mumon-kan)*, translated and with a commentary (San Francisco: North Point Press, 1990), pp. 7–18.

2. Zenkei Shibayama, *Zen Comments on the Mumonkan* (New York: Harper and Row, 1974), pp. 19–31.

3. Kōun Yamada, *Gateless Gate: Newly Translated with Commentary* (Tucson: University of Arizona Press, 1990), pp. 11–16.

Poetry

1. W. S. Merwin and Sōiku Shigematsu, *Sun at Midnight: Poems and Sermons of Musō Soseki* (San Francisco: North Point Press, 1989). A masterful translation of the great poet of the mountains of early Japanese Zen Buddhism.

2. John Stevens, *One Robe, One Bowl: The Zen Poetry of Ryōkan* (New York: Weatherhill, 1988). The endearing, gentle songs and haiku of the Sōtō Zen hermit who couldn't stay away from people.

3. ————, *Mountain Tasting, Zen Haiku by Santōka Taneda.* (New York: Weatherhill, 1980). Tragic, humorous poetry by a medieval poet unluckily born in modern times.

4. R. H. Blyth, *A History of Haiku*, 2 vols. (Tokyo: Hokuseido Press, 1963–64). Perhaps the best introduction to haiku. See I: 105–29, 243–67, 349–427, and II: 46–78, for surveys of the lives and poetry of the four great haiku poets: Bashō, Buson, Issa, and Shiki.

5. Robert Aitken, *A Zen Wave: Bashō's Haiku and Zen* (New York: Weatherhill, 1978). Talks on the Zen Buddhist implications

of Bashō's work. See the first two chapters for a sample of this work.

Legend as Zen Buddhist Teaching

Mou-lam Wong, *The Sutra of Hui Neng,* in *The Diamond Sutra and The Sutra of Hui Neng* (Berkeley: Shambhala, 1969). The "Platform Sutra" in the popular version — the folkloric, instructive story of the Sixth Ancestral Teacher. The autobiography: pp. 11–24. See Philip B. Yampolsky, *The Platform Sutra of the Sixth Patriarch* (New York: Columbia University, 1967) for historical perspectives of Hui-neng's story, pp. 58–88. See Aitken, *The Gateless Barrier,* pp. 19–27, 31, 160–65, and 255–60, for Zen Buddhist teaching found in folklore and dreams.

Sutra Study

1. Garma C. Y. Chang, *The Buddhist Teaching of Totality: The Philosophy of Hwa Yen Buddhism* (University Park: Pennsylvania State University Press, 1977). A comprehensive survey of Hua-yen thought and its foundations, altogether readable. "Fa Tsang's Hall of Mirrors," pp. 22–24, offers an interesting introduction.

2. Thomas Cleary, *Entry into the Inconceivable: An Introduction to Hua-yen Buddhism* (Honolulu: University of Hawaii Press, 1983). A cogent presentation, with translations of classical commentaries. Take it in small chunks, beginning with the introductory chapter.

3. Seikan Hasegawa, *The Cave of Poison Grass: Essays on the Hannya Sutra* (Arlington, Va.: Great Ocean Publishers, 1975). Down-to-earth comments on the Heart Sutra and its impli-

cations and its connections with kōan study. Poorly edited, but nonetheless persuasive. A Rinzai view.

4. Trevor Leggett, *The Tiger's Cave: Translations of Zen Texts* (London: Routledge and Kegan Paul, 1977). Pages 17–125 are devoted to an endearing commentary on the Heart Sutra by Abbot Obora, an otherwise unidentified Sōtō master.

5. A. F. Price, *The Diamond Sutra*, in *The Diamond Sutra and The Sutra of Hui Neng* (Berkeley: Shambhala, 1969). Not a very good translation, it seems, but the most accessible and available.

The Life and Teachings of the Buddha

1. Hajime Nakamura, *Gotama Buddha* (Los Angeles: Buddhist Books International, 1977). What we know and don't know about the life and times of the historical Buddha. A trustworthy study with a Mahayana viewpoint. For the Buddha's first teachings, see pp. 74–80.

2. Walpola Rahula, *What the Buddha Taught* (New York: Grove Press, 1959). The enduring introduction to the basic ideas of the historical Buddha, from a Theravada viewpoint. The Four Noble Truths are discussed on pp. 16–50.

Other References

1. Chang Chung-yuan, *Original Teachings of Ch'an Buddhism* (New York: Pantheon, 1969). Translations from the *Ch'uan-teng lu* (*Dentōroku, Transmission of the Lamp*), classic Chinese compendium of Zen dialogues and stories. See especially the dialogues of Chao-chou Ts'ung-shen (Jōshū Jūshin) and Yün-mên Wên-yen (Unmon Bun'en), pp. 164–73, 283–95.

2. Heinrich Dumoulin, *Zen Buddhism: A History*, vol. I, *India and China* (New York: Macmillan, 1988); vol. II, *Japan* (1990). A valuable, complete reference work, with appendices including a chronological table, a table of Chinese and Japanese names with ideographs, genealogical tables, and indexes of names, terms, and subjects. Chao-chou and Yün-men can be found in I: 167–68, 230–33.

3. Isshū Miura and Ruth Fuller Sasaki, *Zen Dust: The History of the Koan and Koan Study in Rinzai (Lin-chi) Zen* (New York: Harcourt, Brace and World, 1966). The text tends to be technical, but the notes, which compose more than half the book, are full of fascinating information and good stories, readably presented. Chao-chou and Yün-men can be found on pp. 160–61, 249–51.

4. Nancy Wilson Ross, *Buddhism: A Way of Life and Thought* (New York: Random House, 1980). A good first book of Buddhism. The Zen section appears on pp. 141–73.

ABOUT THE AUTHOR

Robert Aitken was first introduced to Zen in a Japanese internment camp during World War II. R. H. Blyth, author of *Zen in English Literature*, was imprisoned in the same camp, and in this setting Aitken began the first of several apprenticeships. After the war Aitken returned often to Japan to study. He became friends with Daisetz T. Suzuki and studied with Nakagawa Sōen Rōshi and Yasutani Haku'un Rōshi. In 1959 he and his wife, Anne, established the Diamond Sangha, a Zen Buddhist society with headquarters in Hawaii. Aitken was given the title "Rōshi" and was authorized to teach by Yamada Kōun Rōshi in 1974; he received full transmission from Yamada Rōshi in 1985. He continues to write, teach, and practice in Hawaii, where he has lived since the age of five.